Protecting Profits in <u>Any</u> Economy

12 Things Your CPA Didn't Tell You about Managing Your Business

Don Crist

Protecting Profits in Any Economy

IBSN #1441499229

EAN 13 #9781441499226

Dedication:

To the thousands of small business owners who risk everything - every day - to meet a payroll; and to deliver products and services we all need.
To those who know the struggle, and who meet their obligations to family, community, employees, and customers, I salute you all!

Protecting Profits in Any Economy

Forward

Don Crist has been a small business consultant for many years having worked for consulting entities and for his own consulting company. A business owner and employee in a variety of industries, he became a consultant because of his love for teaching others the excitement of successful business practices. He has guided business executives from a variety of industries, including: entertainment, political, government, automotive, engineering, retail, agricultural, information technology, chemical manufacturing, stone products, flooring, restaurant, recreation, petroleum, manufacturing, wholesale and retail gardening and landscaping, heating and air-conditioning, roofing, and other building trades. He is a resident of rural Washington Parish, Louisiana and can be personally contacted by e-mail at: pcc@aboutbizhelp.com. Readers are invited to visit the author's website at www.aboutbizhelp.com.

The author does not profess to be the inventor of any of the concepts outlined in these pages, but has used the concepts privately and offers them in this binding to provide tools for business owners to use in managing profitable entities. Several of the charts and tables were given to the author by others sharing files. In the chain of events, it would be difficult to offer acknowledgement to any single individual for file development as many changes have been added to originals passed from one individual to another.

The author is cognizant of the roles legal and accounting professionals perform in assisting small business owners. Expertise they provide is built upon years of education and experience and is not offered here to diminish their roles or significance in providing valuable services to their clients. Legal and accounting professionals are important team members to the owners of small businesses who would find it difficult to navigate the business community without them. Rather, <u>it is to demonstrate the responsibilities business owners have to acquire knowledge about business fundamentals and to offer some basics for their individual use</u>.

Introduction

I've worked for others most of my life, and found a great deal of satisfaction in building business for my employers. When given the opportunity to develop new and creative businesses, I was the guy to help take the steps necessary to get from point A to point B.

My first business ownership venture was to establish a company to manage the aquarium in the Petroleum Industries Pavilion for the 1984 Louisiana World's Exposition. Next, there was a neighborhood grocery store near a public housing complex. The aquarium project was great but resulted in personal financial disaster, while the grocery was successful and sold for a profit after just 6 months. I have since worked for others and myself in a variety of public and private business ventures.

People come to me to ask advice or to plan functions. I can schedule a workday at church or write a successful grant application for a public entity. I've met with the US Secretary of Transportation to get a federal reimbursement for a project – and I got it! I've visited with a US President on Air Force One. I've served on boards and committees with elected officials from New Jersey to Colorado to Texas – working to change or support national policy.

I became a small business consultant and coached CEO's in 52 different cities throughout North America, advising them on business procedures and establishing profitable changes. I can write or design a successful marketing campaign for any type of business. I've written grant applications, policy and procedure manuals, disaster recovery plans, "white papers" on social issues, advertising and direct mail copy, and more. In one instance, a single change I implemented increased business revenue from $25,000 to $40,000 a month without spending a penny.

So, I've undertaken to write some basic business principles into a book for others as a service which they may find useful. My travels brought me into businesses where the owner was experiencing some change which created a problem in cash flow or profits.

The first time I was confronted with a situation of this type, it was with an owner of a small IT consulting business. He had a number of clients who relied on him for software modifications to personalize their individual accounting systems. He sent me his resume and suggested he needed to get a job because his revenues had fallen to a point *where he feared he would go broke. There was a sales tax change on the horizon, so I asked him if he had contacted his clients about the upcoming change. A few weeks later, he called to tell me that by contacting his established clients on this one subject, he was able to pick-up $70,000 of additional business from other projects they needed, but had put off scheduling until they heard from him. He told me not to send out his resume. He was too busy working his business and enjoying his new-found revenue.*

While I'm comfortable with executives in any type of business, my writing is directed primarily to the tradesman who has become an owner, sometimes by necessity or even by accident. For example, he may be a good mechanic who begins doing work evenings and weekends in his garage at home. He acquires tools and equipment to perform these jobs over several years. One day, a neighbor has a verbal confrontation with one of his customers who parked in front of the neighbor's home, and the next thing he knows, a code enforcement officer is at his front door citing him for violating zoning regulations.

So the equipment and tools are moved to a commercial area for a small rent, and a business has begun – by accident, but in earnest. He could just as easily have quit performing side work, but chose instead to escalate and become his own boss. But now he has another problem. He has to manage the _business_. Soon he has employees to pay and needs invoices and application forms. His bank wants a business Tax Identification number and copies of his state and local incorporation or trade name registration. To get paid, he needs to be able to accept credit cards.

He has never considered himself a "businessman." He needs help. He needs someone to speak with about permits and taxes and things he has never considered. He seeks help but finds "vultures" ready to take his money without educating him on the things he needs to know to be successful. $1,000 here and $1,000 there and pretty soon he's questioning this great decision to become self-employed. The Tax Collector visits him and tells him about sales taxes he must collect and remit. He receives a packet about 941 taxes and is really concerned.

Sure he knows his own trade. He knows the suppliers and even the customers. He can fix anything automotive, but he knows nothing about accounting beyond his own checkbook. "What's marketing? I have a sign!" He needs help!

The lawyer will secure his entity and state filings for $800. The CPA will find him a bookkeeper who charges $400 monthly and, for an additional set of fees, will handle his quarterly and annual tax filings. This is customary. But who will help him manage the business and organize his operation for growth. Before, all the money was extra. Now it's all going back out to pay rent, phone, yellow pages advertising, fees, permits, taxes, suppliers, etc. He works on cars all day long – interrupted by telemarketers and drop-in salesman. Then he begins doing paperwork *after hours* until he realizes he's working harder and with less net income. He isn't quite sure how to know if he's charging enough for labor and materials. When confronted with a job to price, his fear is that the customer will go elsewhere if his price is too high. His private customers came to him to save money. Should he continue to charge the same rates as in his garage at home, or charge what the dealerships are charging? Will he get customers if he charges what they do? Will he be able to pay the bills if he doesn't?

The following pages offer some assistance to this tradesman, or to anyone taking the step to become a business owner. You may be considering owning a business in the industry in which you are currently working; or something entirely new. Maybe you want to take on a part-time venture to see if it will pan-out into a full-time opportunity. It doesn't matter which path you choose to establish your own business. What matters is that you establish it on a good foundation. Understanding the principles in this book will enable you to manage your business with an understanding of what it takes to be successful.

Four broad categories exist in establishing and operating any business. They are:

1. **Finance**, the foundation of any business, establishes the sources of revenue, the costs of generating sales, the overhead, and the profit of the business.
2. **Management** offers the method of setting business goals and steps necessary to accomplish them.
3. **Organization** is the pattern of employee distribution and qualifications needed to make your business successful.
4. **Business Development** or Sales is the key to everything because without sales, you have no business.

Every business is first and foremost a sales organization. A contractor who builds homes must have a customer for that home. (I would be the first to admit that many homes are built on speculation. The "spec" home is built and then advertised for sale. But a sale is required for the builder to realize a profit. And the only reason to be in business is to realize a profit.) A retailer must have customers to purchase his goods. An engineer must have a client who contracts for his service. A lawyer, a CPA, an auto mechanic, a machinist, all must have sales to be in business.

But more businesses fail each year because of a failure to understand finances than for any other reason. And, no one can <u>control</u> the destiny of his/her business without an understanding of the financial concepts of the business.

Starting a new business? Growing a business? Read the following chapters to guide you to success at protecting profits in <u>every</u> economic climate.

Table of Contents

Section One: Protecting Profits

Chapter 1. Finance

A. Accounting System

What Accounting system should you use? Most small businesses use some version of **QuickBooks®** to record financial transactions. QuickBooks® has become versatile enough to accommodate almost any type of business, establishing even Point of Sales (POS), multi-user, and bar code systems. Reports are thorough and useful with sample companies and walk-through interviews to establish the operation of your financial package. It's available at most office supply stores and inexpensive for the single-user versions. If you have never used an accounting system, you can still use a simplified version of QuickBooks® because much of the input records are similar to using a checkbook. There are payroll capabilities and tax planning features. I don't work for Intuit, the company which owns QuickBooks® software, but I use it and have seen it used in businesses across America and Canada.

Unfortunately, many businesses begin by the "checkbook" method of accounting. And, some very successful operations continue for many years employing this very same method.

I was once told by a business owner that his secretary brings him all of the bills on the 10th of the month, with the oldest on top and the newest on the bottom. He then writes checks until he runs out of money. He returns the left-over bills to her for next month. Periodically, he runs out of bills before he runs out of money. He calls that profit!! He has run his business this way for many years and continues to do so. And this is no <u>little</u> business. His revenues have grown to exceed $3 million annually.

A ledger system was common before computers were developed. List each transaction in a ledger with six columns (like a checkbook) with one column each for number, date, description, income, expense, and balance. But reports (other than balance) will have to be assembled using the ledger system. Each column would have to be totaled and then a report prepared showing the weekly, monthly, quarterly, and annual totals.

I once used a ledger system for a small grocery I owned. It was quite handy and required my making daily entries. We didn't have a computer, and the categories were broad enough to limit my bookwork. I could visualize each occurrence as the business grew. Each new product added brought new revenues which made my excitement grow as I did the daily entry. But again, each report had to be generated by hand, and sometimes with manual errors which had to be corrected. Closing the month was time consuming and interfered with family and personal time which was far too scarce, anyway. I never had to assemble a balance sheet, but it would have been difficult using the ledger system.

No matter which system of accounting you choose, all accounting is designed to produce reports on finance. How much did you sell? How much did you spend? How much do you owe? How much is owed to you? These answers are contained in the reports gathered from your accounting system. A checkbook doesn't answer all of these questions. So you should choose a package or system which gives you all of what you need.

I recommend that every person investing resources in any business today, purchase a computer and purchase an accounting system. You need the reports to watch your finances and to gather the information you need to make "fact-based" decisions.

QuickBooks® divides its home page into four sections: Vendors (those whom you pay); Customers (those from whom you receive money); Employees (payroll); and Banking (checking, savings, and credit cards).

Chapter 2. Benchmarks – Key Indicators

Every business owner I have met has a series of benchmarks to manage his business. Using these benchmarks, they know instantly if business is good or bad – even before the "bean counters" can tell them.   The accounting people are disappointed that their news is not of more significance, but the owner has different benchmarks and has already surmised the answers contained in the financial reports.

Once I saw the owner of a Laundromat dancing around the room. I asked him what he was celebrating. He told me he had just received the <u>highest</u> water bill he had ever received! It was a new record!!! When I looked puzzled, he explained that when he had a big water bill, he always found more quarters in his machines. This was his highest water bill. Guess what? It was also his biggest month for cash deposits.

Another business owner has a magnetic board which lists rental vehicles in his fleet. He moves markers from one column to another to show what is in the yard, at the shop, or out on rental. He knows that when a vehicle leaves his yard, he is

21

generating revenue. So when the board shows vehicles in the yard, he works like crazy to get them out. When the board shows his vehicles are all out, he worries he won't have enough vehicles to meet the demand. In other words, his awareness of the fleet status gives him a benchmark to recognize the activity level of his business.

These visual indicators help an owner until he becomes comfortable with financial reporting. They are helpful but not complete. In other words, he has no other benchmarks to measure anything but revenue activity from looking at the fleet. He doesn't know if his labor costs are changing, or maintenance costs rising on a particular vehicle. There are more indicators to consider when watching a changing economy. If you want to stay competitive and viable, you must review them all.

Chapter 3. Cash Sales

Some don't like to account for all sales, thinking they are beating the government out of taxes. But what they are really beating is their own ability to understand the important financial aspects of their business.

I once was outside of a lounge in Houston, TX with the owner of a business from another state. He lamented the poor lounge owner's system of having a separate cash register to collect cover-charges at the door. "The poor guy." he said, "He has to report all that cash."

I was called to a business in Florida by a woman who was becoming ill from tension over her husband's business practices. He was claiming $145,000 in annual business revenue when he actually was performing a cash business of nearly that amount each month. Tractor trailers loaded with materials were arriving by the hour. He had five forklifts in motion as materials were being shifted around his brand new 6,000 square foot warehouse. His attitude was one of astonishment that his wife would have any concerns. He wanted no part of any consultant's view of managing his

23

business. I am sure by now he has been introduced to an IRS agent (not by me). All it takes is a disgruntled employee to drop a dime and the penalties are usually more than the dodge was worth. Meanwhile, his wife was envisioning a prison term since she was co-signing the returns which she knew were false! As I said, she was ill because of it.

The only way to truly know what is happening in your business is to account for all money going in and all money going out. No matter the system, you must be knowledgeable about the costs and revenues – especially now, in this economic environment. Regardless of your political, governmental, or regulatory attitude, you can find a **legal** mechanism to **_avoid_** a lot of taxes and some fees once you know what is happening in your business. Being successful is more important than one single expense of your entire business. Every transaction can become a decision of conscience. Ring it up? Don't ring it up? Every cash transaction could cause you a dilemma. My answer is to ring it up so you will have an accounting of it. I'm not telling you this because I am concerned IRS will investigate me. I am saying this because you can later make fact-based decisions to protect profits and your business security.

One client kept some cash sales transactions to pay cash to certain laborers. Both items created problems, in that the cash transactions left deficits in the accounting reports with balances remaining in accounts receivable; while laborers were being paid without any record of their work. The owner didn't know which receivables were a "wink", and which were collectable, relying on the customers to tell him. Payroll was deflated and the owner had to always compensate for the "cash deals" he had made with various employees. Variable weekly hours were a nightmare when computing cash payroll needs. Friday was always a surprise to see if sufficient cash was available to pay those workers and usually resulted in mad dashes to the bank. There was no grasp of payroll or of receivables. The accounting reports were worthless – and the owner was unable to predict cash flow or customer value with any certainty.

Another good reason to account for all revenues is to secure *financing*. If your sales are distorted, your banker will not realize the full revenue picture and will be less inclined to loan funds to a marginal business. No matter how much you tell him about the *other* money, he has no evidence to support lending depositor funds to someone whose sales don't reflect the actual number. Committees are now common in banking. How does a branch manager convince the loan committee of your ability to repay a loan when you have shown zero earnings for the past five years?

Chapter 4. Chart of Accounts

You need to develop a Chart of Accounts to detail the transactions of the business. Sales, Cost of Goods Sold (COGS), and General & Administrative Expenses (G&A) need to be established to give your reports sufficient detail. When you define sales, it could be simply **Sales**. Or, it could be sales of Flowers, Trees, Mulch, Installation Services, Design Services, etc. You can break the sales categories down to provide more detail to show sales from each aspect of your business.

COGS can be similarly broken down to reveal direct labor, sales commissions, materials, freight and delivery costs, equipment rental, maintenance of delivery vehicles, and maintenance of commercial facilities or equipment.

Gross margin is the amount remaining after subtracting the COGS from the total revenues. This is where the business is managed since overhead is generally fixed. *The real opportunity to manage for profit exists in the gross margin.* If you can control your direct labor and materials used to generate sales, and your pricing allows a sufficient amount for G&A and profit, you should be a profitable company. But any time the gross margin changes to allow for less than you need for G&A and profit, you will experience cash problems and lost profits. We will discuss this in greater detail in the section entitled, "**Reading your Financial Statement**".

G&A can be defined by Administrative Salaries, Advertising, Payroll Taxes, Rent, Telephone, Office Supplies, Waste disposal, etc.

QuickBooks® gives samples of a variety of industries to help define a chart of accounts for your business. But you must have sufficient detail for your reports. And the best way to achieve that detail is through the Chart of Accounts. It must be of sufficient detail, but it must also be properly formatted.

Formatting your Chart of Accounts requires that you understand the categories of reports. You have to know what your revenues are – from all sources. You must know what it takes to build an item for sale or what it costs to purchase an item for resale. These costs, which only occur when a sale is contemplated, are called cost of goods sold (COGS) or Variable Costs. Remember, the entire reason for accounting is to obtain useful reports to manage your business. So, with more detail, you will be able to monitor changes and recognize exceptions –both good and bad.

Overhead is the listing of all General and Administrative (G&A) expenses. These are expenses which are constant and occur even if sales are not made on any given day. They include rent, insurance, officer wages, administrative salaries, and professional fees among others. Utilities and lawn care are G&A expenses. Banking fees and yellow pages advertising would be included here. Long-term interest (amortization) on business operating loans and capital purchases are also G&A expenses. These should be relatively stable from month to month. There may be increased fees one month for an annual insurance premium or for real estate taxes. But by and large, they should be almost equal month after month.

G&A includes some expenses which are flexible and unable to be associated with direct sales. Expenses such as cell phone bills could be greater during construction projects but are considered uncategorized and a part of overhead.

Net operating income is the result of subtracting the G&A from the Gross Margin. If you have sold enough at the right price; and have been efficient in managing your COGS so that you obtained a Gross Margin with sufficient amounts to afford the G&A expenses and a profit, the net operating income will be a positive amount.

Establishing a chart of accounts, which is inclusive of every major category you need to monitor, is essential to effective business management. You don't need to be a financial expert to manage your business, but knowing what is happening financially will enable you to secure your business future through fact-based management decisions.

Chapter 5. Reports

All of accounting is designed to provide reports to manage your business. It is not designed for *tax* purposes only. The savvy business owner will become extremely familiar with the accounting reports *for management purposes!*

5-1 Balance Sheet

What is a **balance sheet**? A balance sheet includes three components.

1. **Assets** – everything your business owns including cash, inventory, real estate, vehicles, furniture, and even "good will"
2. **Liabilities** – include everything your business owes including long and short-term debt and accounts payable
3. **Equity** or Stock Value is everything which is left after subtracting the Liabilities from the assets.

It measures Assets, Liabilities and Owners Equity *from the day the business began until the date of the report*. Bankers usually ask for a balance sheet first when you ask about lending. They want to know what you have in equity to determine if collateral exists to support your lending request.

When added together, Liabilities and Equity must equal Assets in a properly formatted balance sheet.

It would be a monumental feet to re-assemble a balance sheet using a ledger system. You would have to begin in the first year of operation and accumulate the balances for each year, and monthly, to the present. Yet, QuickBooks® makes it a very simple experience and can be printed in just a moment.

Here's an example of a Balance Sheet. You may notice that accumulated depreciation is subtracted from fixed assets. IRS allows depreciation to encourage capital investment. This enables you to reduce your tax liability on a portion of investment the business has made in capital purchases of building and equipment. Accumulated depreciation is subtracted from the total value of depreciable items.

It is important that you realize, a Balance Sheet must balance. This means the assets must be equal to the sum of liabilities and equity. Adjustments to Equity enable you to balance the report. If your business has been good and your assets have grown, equity will increase in some proportion to that growth.

But you must also realize, the Balance Sheet is a poor **_management_** tool. You can have a warehouse full of inventory and have no cash. Yet, the balance sheet will show a positive asset total and equity total. You cannot meet payroll with un-sold inventory. You must have sufficient cash to pay bills which is not necessarily visible from the balance sheet. While the banker looks for equity in assets of the business, it is not enough to have assets.

I once performed some work for an agricultural entity which had $7,000,000 of assets, but lacked cash to pay for labor to pick the crop. Until a loan could be secured, they were in serious financial trouble. The ability to repay was not visible from the financial statement, yet, the banker lent money under stringent terms because the assets were more than enough to secure the loan. The owner later had to refinance to obtain favorable terms from a different lender.

You must have the ability to manage elements of your business which can change rapidly to affect your profitability. The best tool in your arsenal to manage rapid changes is the Income Statement or Financial Statement. We will discuss that report next.

The Balance Sheet is an essential element of financial accounting and must be available to you when needed. It displays the value of stockholders' interest in the business. And, it is essential to business valuation. An interest may have to be transferred, upon death or sale of an owner's interests, or to perpetuate the business by transferring interests to another family member.

Having an accounting of your long-term debts and assets is an important element for insurance protection, as well. Fire, storm, and vehicle insurance policies all require some accounting of the assets to be insured. To make decisions regarding coverage, an owner must be able to locate the assets which he needs to replace if lost. These assets are accumulated in the accounting system and can be itemized in the balance sheet. When accumulated depreciation is subtracted, the actual value of the equipment can be computed with some accuracy.

So, it has its purpose. The Balance Sheet, however, should be recognized for its usefulness. It is not a great *management tool* and should be reserved for a specific purpose where its value is appropriate.

Protecting Profits in Any Economy

Balance Sheet		2/2/2009	
Account		**Amount**	**Cumulative Amount**
Current Assets			
Cash		14,000	
Accounts Receivable		16,500	
Inventory		12,000	
Other			
Total Current Assets			**42,500**
Fixed Assets			
Machinery & Equipment		7,500	
Buildings		26,000	
Land		50,000	
Furniture & Fixtures		5,000	
Accumulated Depreciation		-9,900	
Other			
Total Fixed Assets			**78,600**
Total Assets			**121,100**
Liabilities			
Current Liabilities			
Accounts Payable		8,000	
Accrued Expenses		2,500	
Accrued Payroll		8,400	
Current portion of Long-term Debt		6,000	
Line of Credit		15,000	
Other			
Total Current Liabilities		39,900	
Long Term Debt		50,000	
Total Liabilities			**89,900**
Equity			
Common Stock		21,200	
Paid-in Capital		10,000	
Retained Earnings		0	
Total Equity			**31,200**
Total Liabilities and Equity			**121,100**

5-2 Financial Statement or Income Statement

What is a **Financial Statement, or Income Statement**? A financial statement is a report of short – term changes which occur in your business. It is the single most valuable tool in your arsenal to manage your business. Getting reports weekly, monthly, quarterly, and annually enable you to measure short-term changes to monitor each line item for exceptions. If you have a budget (an annual outline of the expectations of management), you can measure performance against the budget to determine how you are doing against goals you established.

- Are sales as you expected?
- Is your Cost of Goods Sold (COGS) at the percentage you estimated?
- Are you getting a gross margin sufficient to pay G&A and profit?
- Is your overhead growing or is it as budgeted?
- Is your net income what you projected?

These measurements enable you to take action to minimize exceptions and deviations from what you expected. If sales are too low, you need to take steps to drive them higher. If net income is too low, check pricing, COGS and overhead to determine if you are performing as expected. If an individual line item changes (such as fuel in 2008), do something to change how it is recovered – such as with adding a fuel surcharge or pricing change. Otherwise, you will be donating the additional expense to your customers who expect you to charge what an item costs to be delivered.

> *I cannot tell you how many times I have entered a business to assist an owner who knew nothing about the Income Statement or anything about its value to management. When one was requested, he would contact the CPA who would prepare it for the use of the owner. The owner would merely submit it to the banker without ever understanding the document he was presenting. Often it would only include Income, Expenses, and Net Income. This format is great for preparing taxes, but not as a management tool. Taxes are <u>only one</u> expense of a business. Management of the business requires that you manage each line item to affect profits.*

To manage financially, you **must use percentages** in your financial statement. You must recognize when an item is greater than budgeted **and its correlation to the sales revenue**. No matter the size of your company, if you fail to proportionately apply costs and expenses to sales, you are eliminating the opportunity to successfully manage your business. Many businesses don't recognize a problem in costs because of an increase in revenue. The profit percentage may decrease while the overall dollar amount of net income increases. When revenues drop off, the problem becomes obvious, but too late, and profits disappear.

Account Name	2007	%	2008	%
Sales	500,000	100	600,000	100
Cost of Goods Sold				
Materials	100,000	20	120,000	20
Direct Labor	125,000	25	150,000	25
Total (COGS)	225,000	45	270,000	45
Gross Margin	275,000	55	330,000	55
Expenses (overhead)				
Insurance	25,000	5	30,000	5
Utilities	12,000	2.4	14,400	2.4
Office Wages	18,000	3.6	21,600	3.6
Officer Wages	60,000	12	72,000	12
Total Fixed Expenses	115,000	23	138,000	23
Net Operating Profit	160,000	32	192,000	32

This example shows what happens when percentages are maintained even with growing revenue. More money is available to generate the higher sales figures (COGS), and to increase salaries and overhead expenses. The percentages remain identical and the business has a greater _dollar amount_ of profit – even with identical percentages.

The next example of an income statement shows what happens when percentages are allowed to "float" (especially due to ignorance of management practices) and how "floating" percentages affect profitability. As the percentages change, the dollar amounts available in each category change, as well. Gross margin is lowered allowing fewer percentage points (and fewer dollars) remaining for overhead and profit. **Managing the gross margin is the best way to manage profits.**

Managing the percentages affords an owner the ability to protect profits regardless of the revenues. If gross margin is insufficient to support labor at 30%, it must be reduced or pricing must change. We have already seen that when percentages are maintained with growing revenues, we grow profits as well. When revenues shrink, we must maintain percentages to protect the profit percentage. Otherwise, we lose funds available to grow equity; or, if allowed to get too excessive, for cash to run the next phase of our business.

Account Name	2007	%	2008	%
Sales	500,000	100	500,000	100
Cost of Goods Sold				
Materials	100,000	20	160,000	32
Direct Labor	125,000	25	180,000	36
Total (COGS)	225,000	45	340,000	68
Gross Margin	275,000	55	160,000	32
Expenses (overhead)				
Insurance	25,000	5	25,000	5
Utilities	12,000	2.4	12,000	2.4
Office Wages	18,000	3.6	18,000	3.6
Officer Wages	60,000	12	60,000	12
Total Fixed Expenses	115,000	23	115,000	23
Net Operating Profit	160,000	32	45,000	9

In the example above, we demonstrated what happens when gross margin isn't properly managed. You must truly manage (by percentages) every phase of your business. Gross margin shrank to 32% from 55% because of changes in materials and direct labor costs. The 23% reduction is *exactly* the same as the difference in Net Operating Profit.

Too often, an owner will look to cut overhead when COGS is the problem. He looks to reduce the fixed expenses when the variable costs are really the culprit. Things like health insurance benefits are reviewed for savings when the biggest culprit is direct labor or materials. Comfort allows for keeping operations employees who generate a product or service. It becomes uncomfortable to remove members of a crew or even entire crews when revenues are flat. But direct costs are where the variables must take place. Some owners will reduce benefits for all in order to keep operations crews in place.

The tough choices made today will protect the stability and security of the entire business for each and every member of the business team – owners and employees. Just be certain that you are making "fact-based" decisions which will truly protect profitability. You must make a profit to remain in business.

To emphasize this point, I call your attention to reports on stock market activities. When a major corporation announces its intention to cut employees (as Microsoft did recently) or to close a manufacturing plant, why does the stock price rise? The reason behind the increase in stock prices is that the owners, or board, took steps to decrease their cost of goods sold to protect dividends (profits) for shareholders. By publicly announcing their intention to protect profits, the company received a "bounce" in stock prices and usually received "buy" recommendations from analysts. More investors are drawn to a company that is taking steps to manage profitability rather than continue to see profits dwindle when revenues contract.

5-3 Variance Report

Another valuable report for management is the **variance** report. Establishing a budget and then measuring each line item against the budgeted line items allows you to see exceptions at a glance. If you budget a payment of $1,000 for accounting and spend $1,300, your variance report will show a plus $300 which sticks out in the report. You can then take steps to investigate the overage and decide what to do about it. It should be reviewed no less often than monthly to show if you are on track to meet your goals. I am not aware of any QuickBooks® report available to show variances, but it may be available on some editions.

Variance Analysis

PERIOD	January		
	Current Month	Budgeted Monthly	Variance Month
SALES AND REVENUES			
Gross Sales - Other	99,472	102,375	(2,903)
Write-offs Bad Debt		0	0
Freight Income	**12,416**	**11,115**	**1,301**
TOTAL SALES	**111,88 8**	**113,490**	**(1,602)**
DIRECT/PRODUCT COSTS			
Plastic		0	0
Freight	8,101	8,325	(224)
Cost of Goods Sold - Other	24,678	28,800	(4,122)
TOTAL DIRECT COSTS	32,779	37,125	**(4,346)**
GROSS PROFIT MARGINS	**79,109**	**76,365**	**2,744**

GENERAL & ADMINISTRATIVE EXPENSE:

Automobile Expense	0	0	0
Bank Charges	0	988	(988)
Building Repairs	318	545	(227)
Building Repairs - Maint & clean	785	785	0
Bad Debt Exp	0	9	(9)
Computer Parts Software Repair	**1,210**	**580**	**630**
Depreciation Exp	1,335	1,335	0
Dues, Fees, Subscriptions	155	302	(147)
Interest expense	126	126	(0)
Insurance	254	254	0
IRA - Employer Match	4,190	4,190	0
Legal & Professional Fees	**1,150**	**333**	**817**
Marketing Expense	352	352	0
Meals for Employer Convenience	2,250	3,988	(1,738)
Miscellaneous	**25**	**16**	**9**
Office Rent		0	0
Office Supplies	**4,850**	**4,735**	**115**
Office Exp - Miscellaneous	**2,680**	**2,355**	**325**
Payroll Expense	91	91	(0)
Postage & delivery	**100**	**0**	**100**
Tax	585	671	(86)
Utilities	**860**	**839**	**21**
Vehicle Lease	3,412	3,412	0
Vehicle Lease		0	0
Wages - Temp	0	72	(72)
Wages - Employee	**39,937**	**39,750**	**187**
TOTAL GENERAL AND ADMINISTRATIVE	64,665	65,726	(1,061)
OPERATING PROFIT / (LOSS)	**14,444**	**10,639**	**3,805**

All items shown in parenthesis are items which have not exceeded the budgeted line items. Bold entries in the variance column exceeded the budgeted amounts and should be reviewed for exceptions to what has been expected. Actually, every difference should be reviewed to determine if something good happened or if something bad happened. The good can be repeated and the bad examined to correct.

In the example above, sales were slightly lower than expected. This could be attributable to anything, even snow in one area of the country. But it should be watched for future trends. Direct Product costs were all lower than expected. Were we using old inventory, or paying less for raw materials? Professional fees and computer parts were significantly higher. The owner should ask, "Why?"

5-4 Key Indicator Report ("Flash" Report

If you could get a snapshot of your business which can be reviewed in less than five minutes, would you be able to manage your business better? Chances are you would be. The key indicator report enables you to review the special elements of your business and to recognize problems within minutes. I recommend that you have a report prepared, preferably by someone you trust with private cash and payroll data, which contains the specific details designed for your business. But don't make the report crazy. Just complete the amounts. Problems will stick out and further information can be obtained to uncover problems. All you want is a report that lists the amounts so you can focus on the problems or realize the good things happening **_at a glance_.**

There are two components to the report - A *Cash* component and an *Operations* component. First the cash side will be explained.

In <u>every</u> business you will need a cash accounting.
- How much did we deposit this week? "Money in"
- How much did we spend this week? "Money out"
- Cash Balance

In <u>some</u> businesses you need an Accounts Receivable section. How much do people owe us?

- New
- Over 30 days
- Over 60 days
- Over 90 days

The owner must become personally involved and <u>may</u> want an attachment to see a list of those over 60 days, together with phone numbers, so he can call each. This is money people owe you for products or services they have already received. *Unless you are a bank, you cannot afford to wait for funds to pay your costs and expenses.* Your profits can be destroyed by others failing to pay you within an appropriate time frame. Retailers are concerned with "inventory turns." What if you were able to make two inventory turns before you were paid? How long would you be able to afford more inventory?

In <u>every</u> business you should have an Accounts Payable section. This shows the amount that you owe to vendors.

- New
- Over 30 days
- Over 60 days
- Over 90 days

You should not have any over 60 days unless there is a problem the vendor has failed to correct. Interest payments or carrying charges can destroy profits and add substantially to the cost of sales. It destroys your ability to work out special arrangements with vendors or to obtain discounts. You have the ability to add several thousands of dollars to your net income every accounting period by managing payables to vendors.

The Operations component includes Sales and Cost of Goods Sold (COGS) entries.

Sales (if done on an accrual basis, this will be different from cash receipts). It can also be broken down by department.

- Cosmetics
- Personal health products
- Detergents
- Meat
- Grocery food items
- Beer
- Liquor
- Tobacco
- Total Sales

Or it could be very broad as only SALES.

Next should be payroll. A substantial portion of your COGS should be payroll. If it varies by overtime, or casual labor, or even seasonal employees, it could change dramatically from week to week. Tax withholding and other payroll expenses should be included in the totals. Overtime is rarely budgeted and can destroy a profitable sale. Pricing never considers overtime unless it is a "special order". By proper scheduling and prioritization of work, most jobs should be accomplished without having to use overtime. If overtime becomes a regular entry, an evaluation of operations must take place.

- Direct Salaries
- Hourly
- Overtime
- Total Direct Payroll

Materials purchased. Whether a finished product for resale or items purchased for building an item for sale, materials are usually a substantial portion of your COGS. They have to be managed, as well. They can be broadly summarized or broken down by component. This section can also be personalized for your business.

- Chemicals
- Equipment Rental
- Lumber
- Other Materials
- Total Materials

Adding these together and subtracting them from sales should enable the owner to see his Gross Margin to know if he will be profitable. If this report is performed weekly, on the same day of every week, with the same cut-off date each week, the owner will have a gauge of every aspect of his business reviewed in only minutes each week. There will be no surprises when monthly or quarterly financial statements are reviewed.

The business can be of any size to benefit from a flash report. Any owner, who values his time away from the office, will appreciate this quick review to allow more time for sales or operations.

As an aside, I have reviewed several forms of "digital dashboards®" or other named software offerings which offer to put this information on your computer all the time. I believe this is too much information, too often. Getting it to work well is difficult enough since it is usually provided by a third-party software company (not your accounting software provider).

If you have a constant view, you may witness major changes on an hourly basis without the perspective of a comparable period or notes from the accounting department. You may become distracted from a priority when seeing changes.

Before an entry is made, the payables clerk may call you to explain that you are about to pay an invoice and not to come "unglued" when it hits your screen. That will distract you before, during, and after the update on your screen! Conversely, you may train yourself to ignore it if it is always on the screen.

The "Flash Report" is designed to be a time-saver - not a distraction to you during production time. It can be reviewed in perspective, at any location, during any hour, on a device of your choosing (fax, e-mail, on-line, blackberry, etc.). It should be significant and anticipated.

From this example of a weekly *"flash"* report, the owner can see his cash position and his weekly operating performance totals against goals. He has a "yardstick" with which to measure his results.

His weekly goals are taken from the annual budget divided by 52. Owner's salary is a part of overhead. In this example, the owner has only one other employee he pays $7 per hour plus labor burden.

Date of Report: (always on Monday or Tuesday for week ending previous Sunday)

Cash	Am't		Operations	Goal	Actual	%
Beginning Balance	$3,500					
Deposits	$6,000		Sales	$6400	$7200	100
Checks written	$4,200					
Cash Balance	$5,300		COGS			
			Materials	$3520	$3660	51%
Accounts Receiv.			Advertising	$80	$ 80	1%
New	$4,464		Financing Expenses		$ 360	5%
Over 30	$2,600		Auto Exp	$100	$ 75	1%
Over 60	0		Payroll			
Over 90	0		Salaried		0	
			Hourly	$300	$300	
Accounts Payable			Overtime		0	
New	$3,600		Total Operations Payroll	$300	$300	4%
Over 30	$700		Total COGS	63%	$4475	62%
Over 60	0		Gross Margin	37%	$2725	38
Over 90	0					

Chapter 6. Management

This chapter is primarily concerned with two things: setting goals for measurement; and obtaining reports from employees, either verbal or written.

Goal setting is really your business plan for the next twelve months. You can prepare something very simple as in a broad budget. You could set broad goals for sales and profits, but the more detailed it is the more measurement standards you will have created.

A famous person once said, "If you can't measure it, you can't manage it." He was right. Another once said, "If you have no goals, you will certainly reach them." He was also right.

6-1 Building a Budget

To measure success, you must have goals. If you need an income of $60,000 you must sell an amount of goods sufficient to realize a profit of $60,000 after paying the cost of producing the sale and paying overhead. That $60,000 is a simple goal. From that simple goal you can back into a budget. In fact, a budget begins with sales or revenue goals. How much can I envision selling this year? Where will my sales come from? How will I advertise my products for sale? How much will it cost me to produce these sales? These are the basic budget questions. If you are a small business, many of those answers are your own estimates. If you have employees, charge them with producing those answers.

Sales:

- My gross profit on one unit of sales is $375; $200 after paying the bills.

- In order to make $60,000, I must sell 300 units.

- 300 units at $800 selling price is $240,000.

- I must sell 6 units weekly to reach my base goal of $4800 to reach my annual goal.

My base annual revenue goal is $240,000. I would prefer to sell 400 units to net $80,000. ___I will set a "stretch" goal of 8 units per week or a revenue goal of $6,400; annually, a goal of $320,000.___ My budget begins with sales revenues of $320,000.

COGS

How much will it cost me to sell the 400 units?

- Purchasing them will cost me $425 per unit or $170,000.

- Advertising will cost me $80 per week or $4,000 annually.

- Shipping is $15 per unit or $6,000

- Financing fees equal 7% or $56 per unit. Annually that would be $22,400 (budget the full amount even though not everyone will finance a unit)

- The total cost of sales (COGS) will be $202,400 or $506 per unit. Weekly, the total COGS should not exceed $4,048.

- My cost of Goods Sold represents 63% of sales.

Gross Margin

Gross margin is what is left after subtracting the COGS from Sales Revenue. Gross margin is $117,600. There is 37% remaining to pay for overhead *and profit*.

General and Administrative Expenses:

What is my overhead? Since I work at home, I have no rent or utilities. And, I'm just starting out and have no employees. So, my overhead is very low. But I do have some expenses.

- Fuel and vehicle expenses of $100 per week becomes $5,200 annually

- My own 941 taxes and FUTA and SUTA will require 15.7% to be remitted monthly or quarterly on my earnings of $60,000 and amounts to $9,400 annually.

- My salary of $5,000 per month is an overhead expense, as well. However, some of the 941 taxes are deducted from my check, reducing my check by 7.5%. The remainder is $55,500.

- I will have office supplies, educational expenses, brochures and printing and other miscellaneous expenses of $3200 annually (1% of sales).

- Total overhead will be $72,800, or $182 per unit.

- My overhead is 23% of sales.

Net Income

Net income is found by subtracting the G&A (overhead) from the Gross Margin. My net Income is $44,800 or $112 per unit. Net Income is 14% of sales, a respectable profit after paying my salary and all expenses.

Having built a budget, I now have revenue goals, COGS goals, and G&A goals which I can use to measure my performance. The ultimate goal for me is the Net Income goal which will be my performance indicator. Can I meet the other goals so I can realize a net income of 14% or $44,800? I will be successful in this business if I can manage the COGS and Gross margin to achieve my Net Income goal.

6-2 Obtaining Reports

If you have no employees, you must do it all. But the minute you employ another person, you must establish a reporting system so you will be made aware of what is going on in your business. The simplest reporting system is done verbally. With only one employee, this is probably ok. But once you begin adding more staff, an established reporting mechanism will enable you to be aware of all that is happening in your company.

If you add a salesman, you will want a report on activity and results. Activity enables you to see the effort being undertaken to achieve the results. If activity is sufficient, the results will follow. If fewer than enough calls are being made, sales results will be insufficient to justify the wages being paid. A simple sales report may include:

- Telephone calls made
- Appointments scheduled – new or follow up
- Appointments concluded
- Units sold
- References obtained

If sufficient telephone contacts are made, sufficient appointments will be scheduled. If sufficient appointments are kept, sufficient units will be sold (assuming basic sales skills).

Each additional sales person added should be required to complete the same report so that you can monitor the activity level of your sales staff. References are the hottest leads and failure to ask for references increases your advertising costs.

I once worked for an insurance company which had done sufficient research to conclude that 50 telephone calls completed resulted in 15 appointments, which resulted in 2 applications per week. They had studied thousands of agents and presented each with a script for telephone calling and a sales presentation guide to follow when on an appointment. Successful agents had used these basic presentations to build a practice and hundreds of clients. For these agents, prospecting became their constant hurdle. If they could get references, they would have sufficient prospects to call and a never ending income stream. This company required activity reporting to gauge the efforts of each agent. The local agency built a substantial client base and became a leader nationally.

In operations, reporting can be just as valuable. Contractors who have several jobs running can gain valuable information from standard field reports comparing work performed to schedules contemplated at the beginning of a job. Every manager and every crew can be monitored through reporting. Customer satisfaction can be measured if sufficient detail is gathered, while complaints and problems can be anticipated through an analysis of reports furnished from the field. The owner may periodically see the actual work performed, but through reports and meetings, will know what is being done on a jobsite, in a factory, or on a sales call.

Meetings are another valuable tool for obtaining information from your employees. A short weekly meeting adds to the reporting mechanism already established. A combination of a weekly meeting and reports may be the best process for larger companies. Priorities need to be established and morale can always stand a boost. When the owner takes time to meet with an employee group, it will improve production and encourage innovation. Frequently, in larger companies, the owner will meet with his managers but not with operations or hourly employees. This is a mistake, in my opinion. I am not suggesting that the owner undermine his manager's authority by making changes or dealing with intra-departmental structure. But hearing from employees who perform the work is valuable on a periodic basis.

I once was called to a manufacturing plant where cumbersome systems appeared to be causing a problem with COGS. Too much labor was being spent in the manufacturing process and it had to be reduced to remain competitive. So, the processes were outlined and the employees asked to offer ideas on how to make the process more efficient. Each step in the process was written on a separate sheet of paper and attached to the wall. Each employee was given a packet of "post-it notes" and asked to write an idea to improve the process. They were asked to step up and attach their "post it" where it fit into the process. The owner was astonished at how many employees furnished ideas and how involved they were in the process. Many of the ideas were good ones which were implemented. The employees themselves were invested in the success of the changes and worked hard to affect them.

Designing simple forms and reports can save an enormous amount of time for the business owner. During a work day, many things occur to distract the owner from priorities. Having production, operations, and administrative reports to review (when things settle down) will enable the savvy owner to focus on matters requiring his attention. He/she can then schedule a time to address these matters with the appropriate employee.

Chapter 7. Process Mapping

Developing a method of duplication is essential for owners to relinquish control and to delegate routine functions of the company.

One method of establishing procedures for others to follow is to map the process so others can see visually what steps are to be taken in performing various tasks. Process mapping enables a company to improve its standards and teach others what standards to follow.

> *One company I visited needed to increase staff. They were prepared to advertise for a position, but didn't know exactly what skills to include in the ad. It was obvious they had not yet considered all of the elements needed before advertising. Business owners don't need more interviewing exercises, they need people to help. So, having a job description of the position to be filled was an essential first step.*

How did we tackle the task?

- Step one was listed as "deciding what *functional* position had to be filled." To whom would the position report?   What skills are necessary to perform the job duties?

- Preparing a job description the applicant could read was next.   The job required driving, so an obvious requirement was a good driving record.
- Physically, the applicant required the ability to climb steps, lift up to 50 lbs, and to operate mechanical equipment. Sight, depth perception, color distinction, and normal hearing were all required. It was also essential the individual clearly speak and understand English for safety and for customer assistance.

Other requirements existed for the position, but you get the idea.

Next, a short list of questions for the applicant were assembled to identify the type of person the applicant might be.

Then, an ad was designed and placed in the local trade journal to attract the person we were looking to find.

Finally, we were able to assign the initial interview to an operational supervisor who would only submit qualified candidates to the owner for final consideration.

By establishing the process, the owner could responsibly delegate all duties except the final decision to other staff members. This process for hiring replacements could then be duplicated in the future without having to reconstruct a process.

Process mapping, once performed in operations, administrative procedures, even simple functions such as opening and closing the business office can be mapped and assembled into a manual for operation of the company. A new employee would begin by reviewing procedures required of the position he/she would fill. Step by step instructions would shorten the time it takes to explain the operational concept to the employee and shorten the orientation period to produce an effective addition to the staff.

The owners' time is freed to focus on more vital needs of the business. Delegation of routine procedures is accomplished, reserving final decisions and methods for the owner.

The process can be refined as needed, enabling the business to gain efficiencies in production, operations, office procedures, and more. It is a valuable management tool which enables an owner to grow the business and expand his effectiveness. Employees can be evaluated on their ability to follow procedures.   Their efficiency and proficiency should be enhanced.

Chapter 8. Organization

Organization, when properly devised, provides the **_infrastructure_** for the growth of your company. If it is defined by function, not by personality, it can be a great way to secure the future. What I'm referring to is the *method of _staffing_* your business.

How often have you heard an employer say the most important element of his business is good people? Truly the infrastructure of a business is centered on having good people in key positions. It is no accident that some companies attract the best employees. They have an established concept of what is needed; defined duties and skills required; a system of reward for outstanding achievement; and an evaluation system to compliment the strengths, while agreeing to work on the weaknesses. They offer internal promotion, recognition, goals and measurements, and competitive compensation, which often include health and other benefits.

Functional Organization:

Frequently, a new business will require the owner serve as President and maybe even the only employee. So, all functions have to be performed by the owner. Later, as revenues grow, the owner may employ others to handle various responsibilities. They may be hired at the manager level or at a subordinate level. But having a blueprint for the growth of your company is very important. Function must be defined so that you will ***fill a position of need rather than hiring a "nice guy".*** You may need help with telephone and bookkeeping before relinquishing management duties. You may need casual labor before adding a permanent operations employee. It's not that you prefer an approach such as this, but the reality of revenues may dictate it. Take the time to design the structure early in your planning process.

- When you prepare your budget, you can visualize the addition of an employee and what that employee would have to perform to justify the expenditure.
- Define the function before considering the person.
- Specify the duties to perform.
- Estimate the cost of the position and the labor burden you will have to add to the hourly wage.

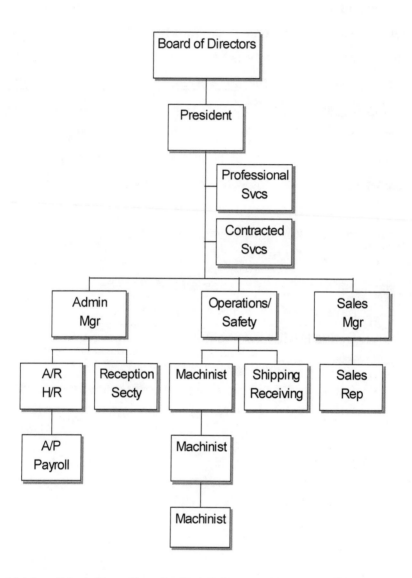

Having this information *before* it is necessary enables you to seek an employee who will be truly valuable to your company immediately. Choices based upon personality would have to be molded to address your priority. They would define a position, but it may not be the position to help your immediate growth.

> *For example: your brother-in-law needs a job, and you need sales help. You need to grow sales in order to justify the addition to payroll, but your strong suit is administration. A new salesman is exactly what you need. Brother-in-law, however, is no salesman. He is wonderfully suited to operations and can manage any number of people and processes. If you hire your brother-in-law and ask him to become a good salesman, chances are, you will have an individual who is just not suited to help you. He will feel that he is not performing well, and you will be dissatisfied. Now, you not only have professional friction, but family gatherings are a disappointment as well. You hired a personality without first addressing your priority.*

If you first:
- identify what you need;
- define the duties and skills necessary to provide value to the company immediately;

- watch for that person to appear, or alternately, advertise for the position;

you will be better suited to affect immediate and sustainable growth in your business. It will give you the blueprint you need to establish a position as growth occurs, so you can manage the growth and sustain it, for the long-term security of employees and you.

Chapter 9. Job Descriptions

You must also design a job description for each position. Failure to do so will allow an employee to design his/her own. Ask any employee if they are doing a good job. They will assert that they are. But they may not be performing the job _you_ envisioned. You need to set the duties to have a measurement standard. The only way to evaluate the performance of any employee is to have a set of standards you designed to measure performance. A salesman may have a sales requirement of one sales unit per week, and a set of activity goals. Ask the salesman if he's doing the job, and now he can say "yes" or "no" based upon the job description. Ask a bookkeeper who must furnish a variety of reports each week if he/she is doing a good job and the answer can be "yes" or "no" based upon your standards. But if you just say "keep the books", the answer may be "yes" while your reports are not available for review.

Employees love parameters. They enjoy knowing you are satisfied with their performance and that they measure-up to standards you have set.

I am in the process of training two young horses. In training horses, you must establish respect for

71

your leadership which comes through consistent ground work. Once that is established, you can begin to add new responsibilities, such as ground work with a saddle. Eventually, if you have done all the steps, you can ride that horse and train it for more advanced commands, feeling secure in the ability of the horse to understand your focus through signals you give. You can build trust and respect for each other's skill.

The same is true of employees. They will respect an owner who establishes expectations and then manages performance in an adult fashion. Your steady leadership and adherence to established guidelines will provide confidence that the job is being performed well and that a mutual respect for each other's talents is being developed. Most employees will attempt to exceed your expectations and will work to achieve your goals. Those who don't perform will be obvious and must be discharged to maintain the respect of those who will.

Having a job description which fully identifies your expectations enables the owner to obtain the right employee, and to evaluate performance based upon standards designed for the position.

Job descriptions for key managers can be elaborate, utilizing several pages of skills required, education and experience measurements, and duties to perform. The job description for a laborer may only list job tasks and duties. Either way you decide to write them, have them in written form to afford your employee the opportunity to do what you want done.

Chapter 10. Incentives

One common mistake made by most employers is that employees will have the same drive and ambition as the owners have for the business. No one cares as much as you do. _Get over it!_ Employees set their own rewards for effort and not all work harder because of cash. I've even heard employers say "How about getting paid for doing their jobs as an incentive?"

I once worked a job where travelling was constant. I left home on Sunday and returned Friday. I didn't see a paycheck for two years. My checks were sent to my home where my wife made the deposits. When I arrived home, there was no discussion of income since my wife had no questions. My satisfaction didn't come from the check, but from the clients. When the "light bulb" went off in their eyes; and they realized the value of the lesson; and could apply it in their own examples; I received the satisfaction I needed and motivation for the next opportunity.

I once performed a consulting engagement for a garden center. One greenhouse was being planted

74

with items that would generate $1 in profit from each starter plant. After showing the owner a method of calculating the square foot value of the greenhouse, he realized that planting and nurturing those plants was a poor use of his facility and time. He could buy those plants from another supplier – earning nearly the same profit - while growing a plant which would produce a $3 profit in his own greenhouse. In changing the plants, he would be able to pay for a new delivery truck in one year as opposed to five years as he had contemplated. Seeing the "light" in his eyes as he computed these changes gave me the satisfaction which provided my motivation.

Once you have a measurement standard, you can establish incentives to drive employees beyond basic performance levels. An incentive is a reward that is **earned**. It is different from a <u>bonus</u> which is **given**. Most employers will award a bonus (Christmas) which is not earned; and bears no relationship to superior job skills or performance. Employees expect to receive the bonus even if they fail to perform to the employer's standards. If it is ever withdrawn, some employees become bitter and resentful. I personally recommend that all bonus programs be eliminated in favor of an incentive program.

An incentive should be designed as a motivation to exceed profit goals and should contain requirements which the employee can measure. A sales goal can be established with the caveat that, once the goal is exceeded, certain rewards will be available. The salesman will be able to earn that goal through exceptional performance and knows what to expect when the goal is exceeded.

It's harder to establish such an incentive for a factory worker, a machinist, or a bookkeeper. I have provided an example of an incentive program which essentially is a no-cost program paid entirely through excess profits. It rewards each individual for their contribution and considers seniority, special skills, level of authority, and evaluation scores. It rewards part-time and full-time differently and includes every position on the organizational chart, even the part-time janitor.

In this example, a variety of factors are included in computing the employee's incentive payment. First, the business has to make a profit which exceeds the target. No excess profit, no incentive. This makes the plan a no-cost program for the business. If you need a 10% profit to sustain the business, set your base at 10%. Our example uses an 8% profit margin before the incentive "kicks in". The excess profits are divided between the company and the employee pool. When added together, all of the points equal 408. By dividing 9,000 by 408, a dollar value of $22.06 can be assigned to each point.

Total Sales	400,000	N/A
Profit Goal %	8%	32,000
Actual Prof %	12.50%	50,000
Excess Profit	4.5%	18,000
Co Share	50%	9,000
Distribution	50%	9,000

Emp	FT PT	Res p	Ev al	Yrs	Sub- tot	Pt Tot	Qtr Incen	Yr En d	Tot Incent
Joe	1	4	97	3	104		1147	1147	2294
Mary	1	3	98	6	108		1191	1191	2382
Phil	1	3	97	5	105		1158	1158	2316
John	.5	1	90	12	52.5		579	579	1158
Suzy	.5	1	77	1	38.5		425	425	850
						408			9000

With $9,000 to divide among the employees, what would be a fair distribution? Our example considers "**Evaluation Score**" as the biggest single factor to consider. If an employee performs below a certain score on his/her evaluation, that employee should not be included.

Seniority is considered as in John's example. John is a part-time Janitor, yet he is rewarded for all 12 years of service. He has consistently contributed to the ability of each other employee to focus attention on their own duties since he has taken care of the office waste.

Joe, Mary, and Phil have similar evaluation scores and seniority. Yet Joe has more **responsibility**. Phil, or Mary, may report to Joe as a supervisor. In any event, the owner has assigned Joe additional responsibilities which should be rewarded above the others.

We add the scores together to get an employee point total. Then we multiply the total by the status of either **full-time or part-time**. A part-time employee who works just Saturdays may be scored at 25%, while a part-timer who works each day may be given a 50% factor.

The goal of this plan is to apportion a larger share of the pool to those who contribute more while including everyone in the pool. This is a fair method and, if done correctly, could produce some very hefty incentive payments. In our example, we considered this and divided payments between the current quarter and the end of the year. If the pool continues to produce rewards of this type, it would serve to be a considerable sum at year end. But an employee who quits would not get the year end amount. It places a reason to stay

(Golden Handcuffs) on good employees who may be enticed by a small increase from another firm.

Remember, not all incentives require cash. Not every employee is motivated by cash although all need it to pay for living expenses. Once basic needs are met, the employee may begin looking for other means of satisfaction. Publicizing an employee's good performance to his peers will often generate his continued good activity. For each, it is a different method. Knowing the owner is aware and is pleased may be enough.

An established incentive plan will enable every employee to grow in desire and accomplishment through exceeding expectations and goals. Collective participation encourages teamwork and gets your employees involved in correcting poor behavior in departmental settings. The chronically late employee will be admonished by peers until he shapes up or is reported to the employer for action. Laziness in the field will be addressed by co-workers who are striving to receive benefits from the incentive plan. Mature employees will recognize the opportunity for better earnings and will not allow some malcontent to mess up the opportunity.

One company established a competition between offices in their company based upon growth. The motivation included a banquet where the winners would eat steak and the losers would eat "crow" (chicken). After establishing office goals, the contest began and each office was determined to eat steak. The owner was able to motivate each office to grow sales and customer satisfaction (2 measurements) without having to pay any cash awards. Employees of every rank were involved in adding to the sales effort. And every employee had a chance to win. No loser had to exist since each was able to meet or exceed the growth targets. Camaraderie was enhanced as communications between offices grew. Yes, it cost something, but the profits were there to pay the cost – and a great deal more! Bragging rights were also established to continue the friendly bantering until the next contest. It was wildly successful and produced a huge growth in sales.

Using non-cash incentives to motivate employees is valuable for the business. While none care as you do for the success you envision, you can still enjoy the positive effects of incentive plans to provide enthusiasm and motivation.

Chapter 11. Evaluations

Each employee having been given a job description can be evaluated. After reviewing performance, a manager should hold a brief meeting with each employee and discuss where the employee met, exceeded, or failed to meet expectations. Often an evaluation is called something different, such as "coaching". The fact is, employees expect to be evaluated and can guess what their evaluation will resemble. It must be positive, in that, strengths and good effort must be emphasized. Weaknesses can be identified with the emphasis on correcting the deficiency through joint effort. Occasionally, an employee just doesn't measure up. For that employee, the evaluation is dreaded until an honest appraisal is given.

I once assisted a manager in conducting his first evaluation sessions. He had an employee who was causing a rift among the departmental staff. The manager had already decided the employee should be let go, but feared the reaction to his recommendation, putting off the evaluation. When I agreed to assist him and we sat down with the employee, it was really very pleasant. We all knew the employee wasn't happy and would probably be better off somewhere else. In fact, the employee

81

offered that he wasn't happy in the first few minutes of discussion. So, the question asked of him was, "What do you really want to be doing?" He responded that he was trying to establish his own business but was afraid of taking the next step which was to resign and do it. We offered him that opportunity and he took it. We all agreed he would be better off trying to achieve his own goals rather than being miserable working where he was.

Performance evaluations are important and another effective means of motivating employees. Knowing they will be scored on tasks, attitude, interdepartmental cooperation, initiative, safety practices, and skill enables an employee to reflect on standards established during the initial hiring process. He/she will, as a minimum, try to perform in a manner consistent with those standards and will frequently try to exceed them. Those who don't can be "weeded-out" for the joy of all involved.

Chapter 12. Business Development

Sales – Sales – Sales – Sales! You have to have sales to have a business. You must sell a product or a service. You have to be a sales organization before you can be anything else. Engineers must have sales to be an engineering design entity. Lawyers must have an hourly fee before they can have an hourly wage. Homebuilders must have a buyer to purchase the home they build. Horse trainers can train all the horses they want, but without customers, they are just "shovellin' sh-t!"

If you don't want to be a salesman, you have a few choices:

- Hire a salesman.
- Joint-venture with a sales organization.
- Work for a salesman.

Selling can be to any market, any group, as long as sales are made and revenues are produced. Some entities have only one customer who pays them as a contractor to perform a service they need. Others have millions of customers – each paying a small amount to generate huge revenues.

I have often wanted to meet with the individual who patented the reflectors used on highways to define lanes. I tried to estimate how many reflectors were being used in a single interstate highway. There

83

must be billions of reflectors on our interstate highways. If each one generated a penny in net profit, the inventor should be a multi-multi-millionaire, at a minimum.

Once you have a selling program and revenues are being generated, you can expand into a variety of markets and add additional products to grow revenues. Getting the revenue base for a new business is usually the most difficult task facing the new owner. Many begin with a built-in first sale which propelled them into the business. Then developing new sales challenges the owner. There are a zillion (?) books written on sales which you could purchase. Many are extraordinary!

Plan for Sales

On several occasions, I have used "Guerilla Marketing" by Jay Conrad Levinson to establish a marketing plan for clients. The seven simple principles outlined were easily implemented and made a significant difference in sales revenues in almost every case. You have to have a plan for sales just as you would every other phase of your business. Sales don't just happen. If you truly want to drive your business, you must have a plan.

Small business owners are usually great technicians who became business owners. They may be skilled at any trade or service and decided to implement that skill in a company they owned themselves. Now, faced with revenue issues, they feel uncomfortable with the sales process and begin to doubt their own ability to sustain the business.

Plan a strategy. How will I generate sales of 400 units per year?

- Advertise in local classified paper offering risk-free trial
- Send out direct mail to business owners
- Hand out brochures
- Get references from satisfied customers
- Find others to begin duplicating my efforts to grow a sales force.

Next, break the steps down into finite numbers.

- To sell 400 units per year, I have to sell 8 units per week (8 x 50 = 400)
- Advertise in local newspapers to get initial leads
- Get references (by offering discounts to those who will furnish references – and call them to set appointments)
- Using the risk-free trial, I have to establish 15 in-home demos per week (3 per day)
- Send out 25 Direct Mail letters each week
- Call those who are sent letters each week

- Establish a commission schedule for those who will sell to others
- Hire one person per Quarter (4 per year) who will sell 100 units each (part-time) or 300 units each (full-time)

General requirements

- Obtain the brochures, business cards and business contact information to establish professional credentials.
- Obtain credit card processing (or Pay Pal), credit financing and other customer assistance tools to complete selling packages.
- Design direct mail cover letters for brochure mailers.
- Obtain supplies.
- Implement Plan.

This is an example of a simple plan to achieve the goal with an outline of steps to take. Each week, an analysis can be done to determine if goals are being met. Adjust your plan to achieve the goals by expanding advertising or sweetening the offer to get better references. Attract others to sell through advertising or through references. You know your own business and can establish marketing plans for your own special brand of skills. They don't have to be 600 page plans with graphs and charts. They can be simple plans. The biggest thing is to have a standard of measurement you can use to determine if you are on track to meet targeted goals.

And, even more important is to consistently implement every phase of the plan. Don't give up if it didn't work the first week. Keep advertising and calling on prospective customers. Adjust the plan to cover different markets or advertising mediums. Adjust your advertising message. Use the internet to expand your market and to ship units secured by credit card. Hire others sooner, or in a different sequence, and train them to get results.

A friend of mine started a greeting card business. The business offers customized greeting cards which can be designed, personalized, and mailed all from any computer. She is adding customers daily. The cards can be used to market any business because everyone wants to get personalized "quality" cards from people they know. It really adds a special touch to any marketing effort. So, every business involved in sales can use her method which has allowed her to grow the business exponentially.

Pre-approach campaigns can be developed which introduce a product, company, or service in a special and personalized manner. Follow-up cards can be sent to reinforce benefits outlined during a meeting. And, thank you cards can follow the purchase requesting additional references. Making people feel special through individual design is a great marketing concept which lends itself to every business.

It doesn't matter which plan you develop, whether a specially designed card or a classified ad. You must develop a system to measure results which can be adjusted to generate contacts for your visits. You must get sufficient notoriety for your product that people will open their minds to the concept you offer. Better advertising will have them calling you to make a purchase, but getting an appointment is the initial goal. After that, a product which solves a problem or offers benefits they need will be purchased by those exposed to the presentation. With enough contacts, enough appointments can be made to result in sufficient sales to meet your goals.

Being in charge of your business includes being able to generate revenues to affect the income (and eventually, the profits) you need to secure your future. By developing even a simple plan, you can take control of revenues.

Section 2. What your CPA didn't tell you about running your business.

Your CPA is a professional who should treat you as a professional in your own field. He assumes that you know everything you need to know to be successful at your business. He does not expect to become your teacher or counselor, or to show you how to read basic reports. So he generally will not explain the following items to you. This is not an oversight on his part. He assumes these things out of respect for your own professional expertise.

You have an obligation to ask questions and to seek guidance. The CPA can be a valuable resource to you. He/she will welcome insightful discussions about most aspects of your plans. But, he will not volunteer a bunch of basic information you should already know. He has too much respect for you to do that.

Chapter 1: **What entity structure should I use to form my business?**

Ask yourself why entities are formed in the first place. There are generally three reasons to form an entity:

1. Liability
2. Taxes, and
3. For business transfer.

So, what type of business are you starting? Will you have a great deal of liability as a result of the service or product you offer? Will your revenues be so great that you will want to divide your income into several "buckets" each with smaller taxable income? Will you later transfer the business to your children or sell it to someone outside of the family?

The answers to these questions will begin to help you determine which entity structure you should employ. I once went to a lawyer to establish a business entity. He suggested an LLC. I asked why not an S-Corp. After his explanation, I still didn't understand why he suggested the LLC. And I still can't determine the value of one over the other for that particular instance. In some states, an LLC is _always_ taxed as a partnership. In others, you can choose other tax treatments. You must, however, accept December 31st as the end of the tax year.

91

Consider Liability. If you drive a school bus and have the possibility that you may one day be subjected to a lawsuit by an injured student, you should protect your personal assets from the assets of the School Bus Business. Even if a little "brat" jumps on top of another passenger and causes an injury, you as the owner/operator will probably be sued. You should not operate this business as a sole proprietorship. You should choose an entity which enables you to separate your business assets from your personal assets. You should separately insure the business, and account for the business revenues and expenditures separately with bank accounts different from your personal banking. These distinctions will provide a legal barrier between your personal and business activities. And, if you operate a fleet of busses, you may want to provide different entities for each bus, each paying a fee to a common management company to manage the various bus companies.

A plumber can be a sole proprietor until his growth requires he purchase additional trucks for crews he hires, or until he works with gas cooking and heating systems. Then, liability increases with additional drivers of additional vehicles and with the volatility of the fuel. He then needs the additional protection afforded through another entity structure.

If, however, you are an artist who sells paintings through a gallery owned by others, you may not need the liability protection of a separate entity. You can be a sole proprietor and keep your accounts and assets joined.

Taxes can require you to consider other entity structures. You may have a business, like a farm, where your products are all sold at the end of the year. You plant in spring, incur all costs by fall when harvest is completed, then sell product until after the New Year. Accounting for revenues and expenses in the same tax year may warrant use of a tax year different from a calendar year. IRS may disallow many deductions for expenses if those expenses exceed the revenues produced during the year. Also, depending upon the entity, you may not be able to carry losses forward to apply against another tax year. The next year, you may be taxed exorbitantly for revenues which don't have corresponding expenses. This could be especially necessary if you have an animal breeding business where markets demand you hold animals for sale until market conditions are best. An entity which affords a different tax year or one which allows you to carry losses forward may be financially better for you.

When income to the business owner is expected to place him in a tax bracket higher than the corporate rate, a C-Corp may be warranted. Various benefit packages are deductible without thresh-holds under the C-Corp. The business owner is treated as an employee and is eligible for different treatment than the sole proprietor. He can receive pension benefits, home rental payments for corporate meetings, and reimbursements which don't carry the same limits or tax treatment as they would for a sole proprietor. Payments for some expenses can be made for the owner without subjecting these funds to payroll taxes - saving 15% on the benefits received.

Another wonderful method of tax avoidance is to establish additional entities with different tax years.

Illustration 1-1

With the graduated income tax system, a greater percentage of tax is paid when more money is earned in a single company. Like a bucket with a small bottom and wide top, tax rates are graduated to take more from those who earn more. If you could earn a small amount in each bucket (company), earnings would be subject to a lower tax rate in each company. The easiest way to do this is to have different tax years and to make advance payments to another company at year end to remove sums from a bucket with more earnings. Both pre-paid expenses and contracts between companies are legal tax avoidance measures. Using this concept is a tremendous advantage to companies with higher revenues and may apply to hundreds of companies who currently pay a high rate of tax.

Business transition, as used in this section, means building the business for sale to an outsider, or transferring the business to a close family member for continuity following the owner's retirement. An LLC or Corporation is easier to transfer since personal assets are not comingled with business assets. It's easier to establish a transfer value, and to make the transfer by selling stock or shares rather than selling each piece of equipment, real estate, rolling stock, inventory, and good-will. The value of life insurance and pension benefits can be determined and retained or sold as part of the package.

One great story I was told involved a farmer whose land had greatly appreciated in value as highway and business development surrounded his acreage. He owned many acres of land and the death taxes would force a sale by his heirs should he die without sufficient liquidity. (And what joy would there be in paying huge death (inheritance) taxes, anyway?) So with the help of a tax planner, the farmer sold his land to his son for a life annuity. The transfer occurred immediately with payments going to the farmer for the rest of his life. The son established a long-term rental agreement with the farming business at closing to separate the two entities. All inheritance taxes were avoided with the son paying the annuity from his earnings (which now included rental income, as well). The annuity payments were not taxable to the farmer, initially, since they represented a return on investment in the first several years of payments. The farmer was later able to take advantage of favorable capital gains rates instead of paying income taxes on the gain. The heir was able to take title to the land immediately with his father maintaining his control within the family business, and all without fear of a huge tax debt. He didn't have to purchase a huge insurance policy to provide liquidity, assuming he was in good enough health to be able to purchase it. The son's entire debt was extinguished upon the death of his father. Separating business activities from the real estate ownership – and the farmer's personal assets - enabled the distribution desired by the farmer while maintaining control over the business of the farm.

Concluding this chapter, I reiterate the entity structure can be <u>very</u> important. A lawyer should be consulted on structure, because of the liability issue. But the CPA you choose will be intimately involved in tax policy regarding the entity. You must give the CPA a chance to provide input so that he/she will be able to make the best "tax policy" decisions on your behalf. Later, tax implications may require additional entities (like the buckets), as may several business components which have high liability value (like the fleet of school busses). Ask your CPA for his input to determine the proper entity structure for each component of the business.

Taxes are relative to net operating income, so the CPA may not be focused on a heavy tax problem for a start-up or small business. When you speak of transition, however, the CPA will understand you have a long-range plan and goals you are focused upon for the future of your business. He should recognize the value you have put on establishing the proper entity to realize your goals. He should treat you with greater sincerity in his answers to you.

Chapter 2: Cash or Accrual Basis for your business?

What type of transactions will you have in your business? Consider the sales transactions you will make. Are you selling a product or a service, or even a product *and* a service? Will you be financing your sales through a third party, or giving people time to pay you? Will you accept credit cards, use PayPal or some other mechanism to accommodate internet transactions?

These are all considerations when considering what type of accounting method you will use. A contractor will be allowed to draw on loan funds as benchmarks are verified. When site preparations are completed, a payment may be authorized and an invoice submitted for work performed. Equipment rental, materials, disposal fees, and labor will have to be reimbursed in the form of a draw. The invoice will be submitted and a receivable established until the funds are paid.

So, when do you want to credit the sale of site preparation? When you do the work and submit the invoice; or, when you get paid? This is the distinction. **If you credit the sale on the date you are paid, then you are using the cash method. If you credit the sale when the invoice is submitted and**

awaiting payment at a later date, you are using the accrual method. In construction, usually the accrual method is preferred. In fact, in most businesses where a delay exists between the invoice date and the receipt of funds, the accrual method is best. Contractors sell the entire contract on the sale date, and then as the job gets underway, payments are made in accordance with a draw schedule.

A retailer who sells a product at the counter can usually use the cash method of accounting, as could a hotel owner, a plumber, a restaurant owner, a janitorial service contractor, even a gasoline wholesaler. These businesses all collect for sales when a product or service is rendered. However, many of these same businesses offer terms for payment to their better customers and may choose to accrue sales until payments are received.

Useful for Marketing: Take the example of a restaurant owner who recognizes that he gets few customers between 3 and 5 o'clock but is constantly being overwhelmed between 7 and 9 o'clock. He can add an early-bird special to his pricing to encourage early diners, improving his customer flow and relieving some pressure from his resources during later dining hours. Or, consider a retailer who is constantly slower during certain hours. He can implement a senior citizens discount special to encourage additional business during the slow period.

But the business owner from another industry who gets paid 30, 60 or 90 days after the sale may require marketing plans which are geared toward slow periods, also. If he is on a cash basis, he may fail to recognize that sales are made in one period but paid for in another, and may implement marketing plans for the wrong period. Knowing when the sale is actually made is very important to maximizing profits throughout the year. If he is working under the accrual system, his sales would be recorded when made regardless of when the funds arrive.

You must have an understanding of how you will treat your customer for payment before determining which method to settle on. It's hard, for income tax purposes, to change from one to another. So, once you decide, you pretty much have to stay with the choice. From year to year, the value of knowing when a sale occurred can affect marketing decisions, employee strength, and budgets.

You can't choose both methods in the same company. Some companies purchase materials and then perform some type of installation of those materials. In these instances, billing is usually consolidated for payment. But sometimes it isn't.

For example, I once purchased a steel building. I was required to pay for the building upon delivery, and the driver was not authorized to unload it without a certified check. Once the building arrived, however, the erection was billed in stages as completed. The company from which I had purchased the building had two separate billing systems for the two transactions. How they accounted for the transactions was probably on the accrual system, recording the building sale as a progressive payment, but I have no way of knowing.

Common Problem: I have been in companies with accounting systems set for cash but mistakenly establish various reports in an accrual format. The owner looks at the reports and criticizes the bookkeeper for leaving recent items out of the report. Both end up blaming the software, calling it a "glitch", while the real culprit is the accounting system and the report settings for either cash or accrual.

You must establish the method of accounting based upon a serious discussion with your CPA. Don't let him/her assume the method. Discuss it to arrive at the appropriate method. Make certain that all reporting systems are based upon this method so accurate reporting will be done.

Chapter 3. Establishing a Chart of Accounts for Your Business

Accounting systems are designed to organize finances in order to make "fact-based" decisions. These decisions must be fact-based to insure the viability of the business and your future income. The Financial Statement offers a report of your finances and may be organized in a variety of methods. The Chart of Accounts sets the organization pattern and outlines the categories which will be detailed.

A CPA is always concerned with taxes (which are usually the client's hot-button, as well) and will frequently organize your chart of accounts, especially with new businesses, into three categories: Revenue, Expenses, and Net Income. This is sufficient for tax preparation, but fails the business owner by depriving him of the best management tool he has. ***Remember, taxes are a single expense of business and should not be the foundation for making management decisions.*** The financial statement, when properly organized, affords a business owner accurate reports with which to make the fact-based decisions he requires. The Chart of Accounts, when properly designed, will organize the financial data into categories with sufficient detail to *measure* his operations. *"**If you can't measure it, you can't manage it!**"*

A proper financial statement, for an LLC, S-Corp, Partnership, or Sole Proprietorship is designed with *Five Categories*:

1. **Income, Sales or Revenue** – This includes all revenue to the business which includes sales, vendor refunds, commissions and bonuses from vendors, etc. Sales discounts are subtracted from revenues before the total is shown.

2. **Cost of Goods Sold** (also called Direct Costs or Costs) – These expenditures include any item which is increased because of a sale. Sales commissions or labor; Workers' Compensation Insurance for production workers, materials used in manufacturing a product; inventory purchases for resale; maintenance of equipment used in production; transportation, fuel and repairs of transport vehicles; Seed and fertilizers in agricultural production; boxes and packaging; inbound freight; chemicals, ink or toner used in printing; travel, meals, and lodging to remote work-sites (such as in a pipeline x-ray business); and countless other costs associated with producing a dollar of sales.

3. **Gross Margin** – The gross margin is determined by subtracting the Cost of Goods Sold from the Revenues. This is where the business is managed and where

profits are protected. You must have sufficient funds after paying the cost of goods sold to cover overhead AND profit.

4. **General and Administrative Expenses** (also called Indirect Expenses, Expenses, or Overhead) – include all expenses which occur whether or not a sale is made. Some of these include rent, telephone, administrative salaries, employee benefits, professional fees, liability insurance, utility payments, trash collection, computer rental, office supplies. Sometimes overhead or G&A expenses include items which aren't comfortably proportioned to a sale or product manufactured. For instance, a realtor may have greater cell phone expense directly related to a selling activity. Yet, the cell phone is included in G&A. We will show you how it is covered in the selling price in another chapter. Generally speaking, G&A expenses are fixed expenses which occur "24-7". They don't have a relationship to a specific sale even though none of them would exist without sales.

5. **Net Operating Income** – is the result of the G&A subtracted from the Gross Margin. It represents the **profit** of the company after all expenses and costs have been paid. It is the single reason to be in business and is the result of fact-based decision

making. Occasionally, accidents happen. But sustained businesses only exist because of proper management. Having a well-defined chart of accounts is the first step to achieving detailed management reports with which to make fact-based decisions.

To demonstrate how a chart of accounts should be constructed, an example is provided below of a Network Marketing (Multi-Level Marketing **MLM**) Business such as Amway or EcoQuest. I chose this industry because of the various revenue sources necessary to include. An insurance sales agency may have an equally vast income category, as would a cosmetic sales company.

Example of a Chart of Accounts for a network marketing (multi-level marketing - MLM) business:

1. Sales
Revenue on sales
    Wellness Product Sales
    Make-up/Skin Products
    Air Purifiers (portable)
    Installed Products
    Water Purifiers
Overrides on sponsored down-line
Bonus Revenue
Vendor Refunds
Sales Taxes Collected
    State
    Local
Non-Sales Income
    Interest Income

Investment Income

2. Cost of Goods Sold

Purchases of Inventory for Resale
  Wellness Products
  Make Up/Skin Products
  Air Purifiers
  PowerwoRX
  Water Purifiers
Brochures and Printing
Financing (customer purchases) Expenses
  Credit Card Discounts
  Financing Discounts
Commissions (1099) Paid to Others
  Susie
  Carol
  Jiffy Cleaners
Demonstration Expenses
  Food & Beverage
  Door prizes
  Room Rental
Referral Expenses/Bonuses Paid
Sales Taxes Paid
  State
  Local
Travel
  Mileage Expenses
  Public Transportation
  Tolls & Parking
  Meals & Coffee while traveling

3. Gross Margin (Sales minus COGS)

4. General & Administrative Expenses (Overhead)

Owners' and Administrative Wages
Performance Bonuses
941 Payroll Taxes
Advertising
  Newspaper
  Direct Mail
  Internet
  Lead Purchases
Amortization Expenses

Banking Expenses
Casual Labor
Conference Expenses/Education
  Books and Periodicals
  Travel
  Meals
  Registration
  Local Transportation
  Material Purchases
Computer
  Web host/DSL
      Web Site Maintenance
  Software
  Hardware x-tras (chords, router, etc)
  Printer Supplies and Ink Jets
Education
  Publications
  Books
  CD's/DVD's
Insurance
  Key Man Life
  HSA Accounts
  Health & Accident Premiums
Professional Services
  Legal
  Accounting
  Consulting
Rent/Office Expense
Office Supplies
Janitorial
Grounds Maintenance/Lawn
Telephone
  Cell Phone
  Land Line
  Fax Line
Trash Collection
Utilities
  Water/Sewerage
  Electricity
  Gas/Propane

5. Net Operating Income (Gross Margin minus G&A)

Since entity-earnings income taxes only apply to a C-Corp, the following (items 6 & 7) only apply to C-Corps.

6. Reserve for Income Taxes
7. Net Income

As you can see from the example, the detail is available for the owner to measure the amount of expenditures by each category, and to determine what costs were incurred to produce the revenues. There are sufficient subdivisions of categories to decide how sales revenues were derived, and how COGS is affected by sales.

In the next chapter, we will discuss how to manage from a financial statement. The statement must be properly organized to allow for **management** of the business. And that means having five categories of entries or seven if a C-Corp.

Remember, you manage the business from the Gross Margin. You must have sufficient Gross Margin to pay overhead (G&A) **and** <u>profit</u>. Using five categories will enable you to visualize the problems with your business so that you can focus on the problem areas. If revenues are lacking, you can implement marketing plans. If COGS are too high, you can take steps to implement efficiencies. If overhead is too high, you can reduce it to protect profits. You have sufficient detail to manage your business. You can establish pricing in accordance with the actual needs of your business.

Later we will discuss other management principles, but having this detail means that you can assign, or **delegate**, various aspects of the business to others. You can assign the COGS budget to an operations manager and review his/her ability to keep production expenses within a (percentage) budget. You can assign the G&A to an office manager to maintain overhead expenses within budget. A sales manager can be trusted to meet revenue goals. Each can then be evaluated to measure performance. If they are able to maintain their budgets or quotas, incentive systems can be implemented to reward performance excellence.

A family restaurant in New York was managed in typical fashion. The patriarch sat before the cash register and handled all transactions. His wife managed the kitchen and cooked the delicacies they offered. His children were waiters while the staff was

110

supplemented by other relatives. When asked why he didn't open additional locations, the owner simply responded with a question, "Who would run the register?" He had no concept of delegating anything as important as collecting payment.

Having a proper format for monitoring finances will afford the owner an opportunity to build an **infrastructure** to grow the business beyond basic proportions.

Chapter 4. How to <u>Read</u> a Financial Statement

To read, and thereby use, a Financial Statement or Income Statement, you must have the statement formatted showing **percentage of income** as an additional column. Any financial statement that excludes or omits percentages is of little value to the owner. Each line item must be presented with its corresponding value (or cost) to the entire document, which the percentage column affords.

Every company – no matter how large or small – has only 100 pennies in every sales dollar. If each dollar is broken into 100 pennies (per cent), you can demonstrate which pennies are required to support the generation of the sales revenue.

The owner or manager must work to ensure that labor, materials, and other "Cost of Goods Sold" line items keep the same percentage even when sales rise or fall. The beauty of the system is that money is affected by the percentage. It affords more cash to pay for labor when sales increase. If the same percentage is applied to the labor budget, more money will be available when sales are increased. It will be in the budget automatically just by maintaining the same percentage.

The same is true if revenues begin to fall. Applying the same percentage of revenue to labor in a falling sales environment

112

will reduce the money available to hire laborers as sales contract. By maintaining the same COGS percentages, you maintain the same percentage of gross margin which is used to pay overhead and profit. ***You manage your "bottom line" (Net Operating Income) from the "gross margin" line item.*** Can you find new suppliers or re-bid existing material contracts? Is there a better way to utilize labor to reduce costs of direct labor? Shouldn't you use less material to construct fewer items?

> *One person I worked with had a business of repairing chimneys following earthquakes in California. He did pretty well until illegal aliens began performing the service for less than his workers were willing to perform. He just wasn't competitive and sales began to disappear. He mentioned his plight to a University Professor who was able to design an insert to accomplish the same stability as the former renovation - without as much labor. He was able to reduce prices, regain his competitive advantage, and regain his business. Through technology, he was able to reduce his direct labor costs to reduce his selling price – eliminating the competition.*

There are expenses in the overhead (G&A) section of your business you cannot control. Insurance can be re-shopped, but it generally increases as replacement costs and liability limits increase. Utilities are a factor of numerous things beyond your control. Again, if sales increase you will have more money available to pay these increases. But if sales decrease, you must manage these line items, as well. Accounting, Receivables, Payroll, and other expenses require administrative staff to handle these duties. When sales revenues grow, you can expand staff with the additional money available using the same percentage of sales. But, again, when sales decrease, you must be vigilant to cut some of those overhead expenses, as well.

The Financial Statement illustrated on page 116 offers an example of a few general line item categories which vary by year of operation. From the illustration you can see that this company was extremely profitable in 2005 but became a break-even company by 2007. The reason for the difference can be found in the percentages. Materials grew from 23% to 35% of sales. Labor grew from 20% to 33%. As these items grew, they extracted pennies from the sales dollar until there were not enough pennies left to support overhead and profit. The Gross Margin shrank from 57% to 32% - a 25% drop. These pennies came from the "net operating income" line item to make up the difference. In other words, profits shrank by the same 25%. Overhead increased by 11% during the same period to further reduce profits. It is obvious to even the untrained eye, that continuing on the same path for even one more year will bankrupt the company. Returning to 2005 percentage levels will insure a stable financial future for the owner AND his employees.

It is also obvious that net income *dollars* grew from 2005 to 2006. This may mask a problem in managing your business unless *percentages* are used. By realizing an increase in net income dollars *even though the percentage shrank*, the owner may be delaying solutions which could avoid the 2007 problem until the problem became apparent at year end. And, year end statements are not always visible immediately. They may be delayed by a CPA's workload. So the owner may not receive the surprise until the third month of the next operating year. By then, solutions have been further delayed and losses are already affecting cash flow.

It is far better for everyone if the owner has access to these numbers each month and adjusts by percentages to accommodate the sales revenues. If you are a new business and don't have access to historical data, you may need to begin with a "projected budget" to measure your "actual experience" against.

Item	2005	%	2006	%	2007	%
Sales	400,000	100	600,000	100	550,000	100
Materials	92,000	23	168,000	28	192,500	35
Direct Labor	80,000	20	150,000	25	181,500	33
Cost of Goods Sold	172,000	43	318,000	53	374,000	68
Gross Margin	228,000	57	282,000	47	176,000	32
Insurance	20,000	5	30,000	5	40,000	7
Utilities	20,000	5	30,000	5	40,000	7
Office Wages	12,000	3	24,000	4	35,000	7
Officer Wages	28,000	7	42,000	7	56,000	10
Total General & Admin (overhead)	80,000	20	126,000	21	174,000	31
Net Income	148,000	37	168,000	28	2,000	1

Another solution to falling profits may be to increase pricing. It may be that overhead increases have not been factored into your pricing. We will discuss the proper method of pricing in a later segment. For this installment, we are concerned with the use of the Financial Statement, Income Statement, Profit and Loss Statement or whatever your report is titled. It must be displayed using percentages to be truly valuable. It must be reviewed timely, and the owner must adjust his/her costs and expenses to achieve the targeted goals to protect profits. ***The Financial Statement is the best tool an owner has to maintain profitability in any environment.*** It is truly a shame to see business owners "stacking" reports because they are formatted in a useless manner, or have no idea how to use them to guide decisions.

A recent study by one consulting firm concluded that the number one cause of business failures in the US is a direct result of poor or inadequate financial reporting. Structuring your Chart of Accounts to give you the financial data you need to make fact-based decisions is imperative to financial stability. Your business and employees require it.

Chapter 5. How a Financial Statement differs from a Balance Sheet

A Balance Sheet measures the growth of your business from the beginning of the business to the ending date of the Balance Sheet. It is a snapshot of how ever long you've been in business.

The Balance Sheet is divided into three sections:

1. Assets are what you own. This is the present accounting value of what you own, what others owe you, and includes your equipment and finished inventory. Current assets are those due you within one year, or "on-hand" items. Long-term assets are those which are due to you over a longer time period than one-year. They include mortgages.

2. Liabilities are those debts or goods you owe to others. Current means within one year; and Long-term means greater than one year.

3. Owners' Equity also called "Net Worth", "Stock Value" or "Ownership Interest" is the net value of your company after subtracting the value of the liabilities from the value of the assets. It is computed by subtracting the Liabilities from the Assets (Assets minus Liabilities = Equity).

118

While your Financial Statement measures how well you did in each time frame (year, quarter, month) the Balance Sheet measures how well you did from the day you began your business. It goes on forever and reflects the current state of owner's equity. That is why bankers always want to see the Balance Sheet first.

The business owner is frequently concerned with rapid changes displayed in the shorter time frames of the Financial Statement, while the Balance Sheet shows the results of many changes and decisions over a longer time frame.

A CPA will rarely explain these differences as he/she furnishes each to you. It is up to you to understand what you're reviewing. You must determine to manage your business and to allow owner's equity to grow based upon smaller increments of good decisions. By establishing your financial statement in the proper format for management, you can manage the pennies so dollars will be properly grown on the balance sheet.

Chapter 6. Why you should establish a budget projection for the New Year

Unless you have a "cross on top of your business" (church), realizing <u>profits</u> is why your business exists. A Financial Statement tells you what ***has*** happened. A budget establishes a plan for what ***should*** happen. It should be organized in the same format as the Financial Statement – and – it should contain *percentages*.

When driving a car, do you drive while looking in the rearview mirror or through the windshield? Running a business by looking back is a certain way to "collide with" unforeseen problems. Relying on a report after the fact can produce unwanted results. But, in business, surprises **can** be avoided. How often have you heard an owner say that his business is running him, instead of him running his business? Have you ever sat in the CPA's office to hear (surprise!) you owe a great deal in taxes? Or, worse, have you heard (surprise!) you don't owe anything because you didn't make any money?

Even if you are just starting a new business, you should have some idea of what to expect. You may need a certain level of revenue to meet your personal salary requirements. Your overhead may be "fixed" at some level and you need to create sales (some amount) to achieve that number.

A budget will enable you to control your activities to achieve your goals. If more sales are needed, implement a sound marketing plan. If Cost of Goods Sold is too high, make cuts or design new efficiencies to protect your profits. If those efficiencies can't be achieved because of some new cost, adjust pricing to accommodate the new expense. Choose to look forward to avoid surprises.

Many business owners are convinced that selling more will solve all problems. This isn't necessarily true. One business I assisted was selling a product for less than it cost them to produce it. It doesn't matter why it cost more, although in this case it was because of inflated Cost of Goods Sold. Volume of sales would never solve their problem. They needed to fix the other problems before growing sales. But the budget would have shown the problem – glaringly. Their pricing was wrong for the expenses they were paying. Without a budget, they just kept pushing more sales and going further into debt. Volume is not the only solution – it is only one solution. A budget will

121

focus your attention on the real solutions to protect profits.

Another poor idea is to sell at cost just to keep your employees busy. Instead, sell excess capacity into other markets for less because your overhead has been achieved in your primary market. You should never sell at cost or break-even in your primary market.

And still another poor idea is to produce a bunch of "finished goods" just to keep your employees working. Remember, every business is a sales organization. Nothing happens unless there is a sale for a product or service. It may look great on your balance sheet to have a warehouse full of finished goods, but unless there are sales for the product, you have built a "palace in the poorhouse."

I once was called into a company that moved from cramped quarters into a new building with a huge warehouse. The owner began filling it up (the warehouse) until he had a warehouse full of finished goods. He had spent his excess funds for *new inventory and had little left at year end. Confronted with an income tax bill, the owner asked, "If I made all this money, where is it?" I asked him to look around the warehouse. His profits had been re-invested and were all tied up in slower moving, high priced inventory. He lacked liquidity to pay his tax bill and had to <u>borrow</u> funds to pay taxes.*

The best reason for a budget is to measure your progress. Remember, "***<u>If you can't measure it, you can't manage it</u>***" – **period!** When you have a budget, you have goals to strive to reach - revenue goals *and* expense goals. These goals can be measured even daily. Sales goals can be broken down to each day and the owner can review daily sales figures to determine if the revenues will be achieved to meet the expenses – and to achieve profits.

Some retailers have gone so far as to manage daily hours – providing a budget for the manager to use to staff the showroom floor during slow periods and higher traffic times. Labor is one of the highest of Cost of Goods Sold for a company. Split shifts and overlapping shifts are used to accommodate the various selling periods to keep labor costs to a minimum. Part-time and seasonal employees are added rather than providing level staffing during slower periods of either manufacturing or retailing.

By having a budget, based upon historical or projected sales activities, you can spend only those **pennies** necessary to be competitive and to make a profit.

> *I once worked for a ladies clothing chain where the owner kept outstanding sales records. I overheard his conversation with a buyer demanding additional inventory of blue jeans to sell during the Mardi Gras season in New Orleans. His conversation (I could only hear his side) went something like this, "Last year we sold 2000 pair during the weekend prior to Mardi Gras. I only have 1200 pair. If you don't send me another 1,200 today, I won't be able to beat last year's sales, and you will cost me my bonus."*

This retailer obviously had a planned budget which was different from the buyer's. He was aware that Mardi Gras fell on different calendar days each year, while the buyer was looking at calendar year sales for the historical time period last year. By expressing himself the way he did, the manager was able to generate the urgency necessary to get the product to sell in time to increase sales for the stated period. Through

124

historical sales records and projected sales event dates, we can budget our expenses to achieve better sales. This retailer was driving his business to achieve his goals. His, in fact, was the top retail store in the chain of this company for many years before his retirement.

> *Another experience was that of a retail grocer who wanted to increase revenues. By expanding his hours, his costs were only for the additional labor since utilities, rent, advertising, (all of his overhead) etc. were already accommodated. By adding a new product (such as beer, deli, hardware or bakery products) to sell, he could accomplish the same result without increasing hours. But now, options exist to grow his business. Through budgeting he can evaluate which option to choose and plan for the result. He can control the decision and his business growth.*

Each year, or before beginning your business, you should sit down and plan your sales and expenses. Many CPA's fail to encourage this process and many businesses fail each year because they lack the measurements necessary to manage according to a realistic plan. Everything is fine during a roaring economy, but let things get a little slower, and you (surprise) start to lose cash flow which is actually your profits. Let fuel prices climb and the once profitable trucking company becomes marginal. Increase delivery costs by 8% of sales and watch what happens to a 10% profit margin.

Choose instead to **drive** your business and to **measure** against planned goals.

- Set a minimum and a "stretch" goal for sales. The minimum would be what you consider the least you can sell while still achieving enough to pay expenses **and** to make a profit. The "stretch" goal would be what you want to sell to increase your profits for the year.

- Divide the "stretch" goal into 52 and you will have a weekly sales goal. Each week, you can determine if you met your goals, and if not, establish a marketing plan or advertising plan to reach the goal. If you do not at least achieve the minimum goal, expenses will have to be cut.

- Establish the Cost of Goods Sold budget for producing goods or services based upon the minimum sales figures. Make every effort to stay within those goals for each week of the year. There will be deviations because some inventory or raw material purchases are better done in quantity, but usually even quantity discounts can be achieved by having the items shipped and billed as needed. If you are consistently meeting your stretch goals while maintaining your COGS & G&A at budgeted levels, your profits will be growing in direct proportion.

- Manage your direct labor to achieve your weekly goals. Your sales and labor should coincide with only a short lag time. You may have some extra labor which will not be accommodated in sales figures for one week, but consistently "missing" this goal will cost you on the "bottom line".

- Overhead should be nearly level month after month. There may be some fluctuations when paying an annual insurance premium, an annual property tax invoice, or when marketing expenses are increased. But by and large, overhead expenses should be generally consistent.

Once you have established a budget, divide the entire document – line item by line item – into 12. This monthly budget should be reviewed for discrepancies called "variances". The variance report shows where sales and expenses have varied over or under the budget. Two minus one is always one. *If you sell what you planned to sell, and spent what you planned to spend, you will have the profit you budgeted - <u>guaranteed</u>.*

You can adjust the line items to meet your intended goals. If one expense is greater than projected, you must reduce another line item to bring the total into compliance. If sales are lower than expected, you can take steps to drive sales to meet your needs. Either way, with a budget, you are in control and not subject to big surprises. You will never be surprised at year end if you manage your business according to a budget, and review it periodically in the form of variance reports. But, more importantly, you can make corrections to individual line items to effect the Gross Margin assuring your profits are being protected.

Chapter 7.   Weekly Management to Protect Profits

The only reason to be in business is to earn a profit. The easiest method of protecting profits is to break the year into weeks, and to manage weekly. Why a week? It is the shortest reasonable unit of measurement for a business. Payroll, work schedules, and any number of other business items are contained weekly. Under the weekly system, a business owner has eliminated the risk of allowing problems to grow.   If financials are reviewed monthly, 8.3% of the year has expired before the problem has even surfaced.   But if problems are identified on a weekly basis, less than 2% of the year has expired leaving the ability to adjust to offset the effects of the problem.

For example:

Scenario #1. Fuel prices go up. You are reviewing financials on a monthly basis and you notice the increased expenditures. By now, you have sales delivery commitments for another week, leaving you vulnerable to continued reductions in profits for even the near future. You have incurred losses on deliveries equaling 8.3% of the year with an additional 2% of the year already committed to the same problem. Making adjustments now will not recover the losses you have already incurred forcing cuts in other line items of the operating budget.

Scenario #2. You recognize the problem (reviewing the expenditures from a weekly key indicator report) and add a fuel surcharge to the subsequent deliveries. You have eliminated the problem for subsequent weeks, allowing you to protect profits on deliveries. The loss incurred only existed for 2% of your entire year, allowing sufficient time to recover or adjust to protect annual profits.

Under scenario 2, the environment becomes a "*risk-free*" environment enabling problems to be identified sooner, action taken sooner, smaller losses to be overcome, and with profits protected.

Another example:

Scenario 1. Sales are falling but manufacturing payroll continues without change. You receive the *monthly* financial statement and discover your direct labor (as a percentage of sales) has grown from 22% to 29%. You call the operations manager and ask him what is happening. He tells you that he has been utilizing direct labor to perform general cleaning and maintenance because they have not been as busy in operating the machinery. Orders aren't continuous as they had been.

You make the decision to reduce labor to better align with budgeted goals. But the damage is done. 8.3% of the year has gone before the problem was identified. Serious adjustments in other line items will have to be made to accommodate a generous operations manager.

Scenario 2. Sales are falling and the weekly "flash" report is presented. You notice the reduction in sales and ask if corresponding cuts are being made in COGS. The operations manager informs you that his crew is the same and that he would utilize them for cleaning and general maintenance until orders improve. You decide not to accept his recommendation (knowing what sales are pending) and reduce the labor costs during the slowdown. Your profits have been protected and the other employees have greater security that the business will survive the slow period until sales are improved.

Key Indicator Report (Flash Report)
So, what is a key indicator report and how should it be constructed? In the concept of management by "exception" or in using "variances" to find problems, you must create a snapshot of key segments of your business which can be quickly reviewed each week. These should be kept in a binder

or accessible on your computer for comparison. Either way, the same elements must be included.

Section 1. There should be a cash report which details your cash position. The example on page 133 allows the business owner to visualize the existing cash position of his business and to notice cash problems immediately.

Section 2. There should be an operations report which details the COGS and G&A expenditures in very general categories. You must know what wages and materials are doing as a percentage of sales. There may be other unusual elements which occur but should be addressed in "Notes" rather than changing the categories from week to week. In other words, these reports should contain *identical* "broad" categories of information. You don't want to get bogged down with minor details unless something has changed (better or worse).

If something good has happened, such as payroll reduction as a percentage of sales, you want to know why – so you can duplicate it again. Maybe the foreman on a job is more aggressive at getting the work done or is more knowledgeable and drives his labor cost down. That effort should be duplicated and even rewarded. Of course, he may also be cutting corners which may not be obvious until after the customer takes possession. Cutting corners should be addressed immediately to avoid maintenance or warranty problems after the sale. The owner should determine why a change has occurred.

Date of Report: (always on Monday or Tuesday for week ending previous Sunday)

Cash	Amount		Operations	Goal	Actual	%
Beginning Balance	$3,500					
Deposits	$6,000		Sales	$6400	$7200	100
Checks written	$4,200					
Cash Balance	$5,300		COGS			
			Materials	$3520	$3660	51%
Accounts Receiv.			Advertising	$80	$ 80	1%
New	$4,464		Financing Expenses		$ 360	5%
Over 30	$2,600		Auto Exp	$100	$ 75	1%
Over 60	0		Payroll			
Over 90	0		Salaried		0	
			Hourly	$300	$300	
Accounts Payable			Overtime		0	
New	$3,600		Total Operations Payroll	$300	$300	4%
Over 30	$700		Total COGS	63%	$4475	62%
Over 60	0		Gross Margin	37%	$2725	38%
Over 90	0					

You can request more detail if something appears different or unusual. When exceptions occur, there is a reason. The savvy business owner simply needs to be able to review the records to notice the change (in the general category) so focus can be directed toward solving the problem. Having the information summarized and presented **_on the same day each week, covering the same period of the previous week, in the same format_** affords comparison which makes change glaring.

With communication as it is, a business owner can receive a report of this type from his accounting staff anywhere in the world by e-mail, fax, or on-line. There is no reason to vary the date, period, or information categories in the report. Some accountants want to expand it to show a change. "Keep it simple stupid" (KISS) principle should apply. Unusual items or exceptional details should be noted in the "notes" section. Don't change the categories or format of the information.

Chapter 8. Can you afford a new capital purchase?

You have built your new plumbing business to where you are working 16 hour days. You're making money but feel it's been at great sacrifice to your family. You make a decision to employ another crew to split the workload and to allow a more reasonable lifestyle for the business owner - you. But, can you afford to purchase another vehicle and pay another crew? How do you know?

To answer your question, let's look at the financial statement. Your cost of goods sold is 40% of sales. Your overhead (G&A) is 30% including the truck you are already financing. Sales have been running at about $20,800 ($70 per hour * 298 hours) per month over the last several months. You assume the new crew can take part of your workload and add enough to fill their time to a full workweek (40 hours). Assuming you can grow sales by 25%, what would it cost to implement the new crew?

- Truck (annual financing amount)   5,000
- Insurance   5,000
- Fuel and Repairs   5,000
- Modifications to truck bed   6,000
- Salary of plumber   40,000

- Salary of helper   25,000
- 941 taxes   10,000
- Worker's Comp (8 %?)   6,000
- Small Tools   3,000
- Parts and inventory   1,000
- Contingencies @ 10%   10,000

Total cost to implement for one year $116,000

Current Sales @ 20,800 x 12 = 249,600

COGS @ 40%   = 99,840

G&A   @ 30%   = 74,880

Net Income 30%   = 74,880

Current Break-even is 124,800

(calculated by using the following equation):

Break-even = Overhead/1-(COGS/Sales)

$$= 74,880/ 1- (99,840/249,600)$$
$$= 74,880/ 1- (.400)$$
$$= 74,880/ .60$$
$$= 124,800$$

For the purposes of our example, add all of the costs associated with the new crew into the COGS part of the formula to determine the new break-even point. The new Break-even point would be $242,333 based upon the same formula (after also adding the increased sales to the total sales volume).

$$\textbf{Break-even = Overhead / 1-(COGS/Sales)}$$
$$= 74,880 / 1\text{-}(215,840/312,000)$$
$$= 74,880 / 1\text{-}(.691)$$
$$= 74,880 / .309$$
$$= 242,333$$

Without profits, sales would have to equal $242,333 (Break-even) just to pay the new costs with existing overhead. The new projection of $312,000 would include a net operating income of 22.3%. **Therefore, the answer is yes.** You **can** afford to purchase the new truck and add a new crew to the business, while enjoying a 22.3% net income on sales.

Your previous profit was 30%. You can achieve a greater quality to your life for a cost to your bottom line of about $5,000 a year. Previously, you made 30% on roughly $250,000. Now you envision 22.3% of $312,000 – a $5,000 difference in net operating income.

This was an example of "fact-based" decision making. You took facts in existence, made calculated assumptions based upon real data, and found the answer to your question. The three musts included in this scenario are:

1. Grow sales by 25%
2. Keep capital expansion within budget
3. Monitor every week to make certain you are meeting the sales and expense goals.

There are Excel tools available to provide the calculations enabling you to test scenarios of varying capital amounts in seconds. But using this method, you can be certain that your decision can be funded and your hours can be reduced, while enjoying a minimal (if any) reduction in profits percentage.

Chapter 9. Pricing your Products or Services

Who should decide how much you charge for your product or service? Unfortunately, many tradesmen and small business owners allow their competition to set the prices. This can be either good or bad for various time frames, but over the long haul, it is a recipe for disaster. A CPA will rarely discuss your pricing structure with you. He assumes you know your business and don't need to ask him how to figure on a correct pricing structure.

You are in business to make a profit – period. Therefore, you must charge enough in each sale to pay all of your Cost of Goods Sold, a reasonable percentage of your General and Administrative Expenses (overhead), and a reasonable profit.

So, if you install a piece of pipe that is four feet in length, along with two elbows, and it took you one hour (including travel), how much should you charge? The pipe and joints cost only $6. The glue was left over from another job. Tools were purchased at another time. So, how much do I charge?

To understand pricing, you must understand how to calculate its components.

- Direct Cost

- A proportional and comprehensive Overhead
- Profit

Step One - Direct Cost (COGS) include labor and materials. In our example, our labor was one hour and our materials were $6. What does it cost us to produce one hour of labor?

    1. **actual labor cost**

        Hourly rate for plumber

        Hourly rate for helper (if one is used)

    2. **Labor burden**

        941 taxes

        Worker's comp insurance

        Any employee benefit costs

Obviously, each hour of workers' comp is figured on a percentage, as is the tax costs under IRS 941. So if we take the actual pay rate for the plumber ($17.50), add the 941 rate including FUTA & SUTA of 15.7% ($2.75), and the rate of workers' comp 8% ($1.40); we get $21.65; then do the same for the helper: $9.00 + 1.41 (941) + .72 (work comp) = $11.13; we find a labor rate of $32.78. We add the labor rate – $32.78 - to the materials – $6.00 - to determine our total COGS = $38.78.

Step 2 - Next we must calculate a proportional and comprehensive amount of overhead for this job. Remember the glue? It came from somewhere. What about advertising, invoice forms, banking services, officer wages, administrative salaries, telephone, rent, insurance, accounting fees, vehicle expenses, fuel, tools, etc? These have to be billed and collected.

The easiest way to account for these expenses is by taking a fixed overhead percentage and adding it to the COGS for the job. So, what percentage should we use? Should we guess? Is it ok to ask another plumber what he uses and just use his percentage? Unfortunately, many do.

There is a simple formula for calculating overhead. But you must have a properly formatted Income Statement to use it. The income statement can be based upon historical results, or upon projected (budgeted) results. If you have created a realistic budget based upon realistic numbers for sales and expenses, you may use those numbers to project your comprehensive overhead (G&A) for the next year. The formula is as follows:

$$\text{Overhead Factor} = \frac{\text{G\&A}}{\text{COGS}}$$

From Chapter 8, we can use the example of overhead being $74,880; and the COGS being $215,840 (as budgeted with the new crew). To determine our overhead factor we simply divide the annual G&A amount by the COGS. The result is 34.69%. Remember this is not your overhead "rate" it is your overhead "factor." This is the *factor* you will use to determine pricing.

Using the overhead factor, you simply multiply the factor times the COGS.

$$.3469 \times 38.78 = \$13.45$$

This is the amount of **overhead** to charge on this one job to assure you are collecting for the expenses required to deliver the service. When added to the COGS of 38.78, the **break-even** price for this job is $52.23.

Step 3 - But you are not in business to break-even. You are in business to make a profit. So we must add the budgeted profit to the job in order to realize our budgeted goals for the year. So, how are profits calculated before invoicing the customer? Again, a simple formula exists to assure you include sufficient amounts to realize the profit you set out to collect.

Break-even / (1 - profit percentage) = selling price

For our example:

52.23 / (1 – profit percentage) = Selling Price

52.23 / (1 – 25%) = Selling Price

52.23 / (.75) = Selling Price

52.23 / .75 = $69.64

You may wish to round the total to $70.00. That way you will make the price more visibly appropriate and still include the amounts you need to make the profit you need.

Why did we **divide** the COGS by the reciprocal of the percentage we wanted? Why not just multiply the COGS by 25%? The answer is that **our profit is a percentage of the total selling price not a mark-up of cost**. Many business owners fail to understand the difference between mark-up and margin. Retailers are more comfortable figuring margin (a product of sales total) rather than mark-up (a product of cost).

In our example, the profit we hope to achieve is at least 25% of the selling price. 25% of $70 is $17.50. Our profit is $17.50 on a sale of $70.

If we had marked up the price 25% from 52.23, our profit would have been $13.05 – 20% of the selling price. We would have questioned why we never made the desired profit under our mark-up system. The answer would be you used a mark-up rather than charging 25% of the selling price (margin). The formula we illustrated above allows you to realize the budgeted profit (25%) on the $70 sale.

In Summary, you must have all of the elements included in your price.

- COGS, includes all costs associated with delivering the product or service;
- G&A, or overhead, calculated from the historical financial statement or better, from next year's budget; and
- Profit, determined by dividing (to get the margin) the total costs (COGS + G&A) by the reciprocal of the percentage you desire.

Your selling price will always include sufficient amounts to pay the bills and to realize the budgeted profit. Once the hourly rate is established for the year (pay rate, 941, worker's comp, etc.) you can use it over and over again unless something changes. The same applies to overhead. Use the same rate unless some change occurs to substantially change the rate.

You can build tables of hours and material charges to enable your crew to collect the amount at the customer's site on each job. Or, you can exercise greater control by performing the calculations for the crew over the phone. With cell phones, management is rarely out of touch with field crews.

An example of the table you may build:

Material Pricing:

Price	Selling price
$1	$1.80
$2	$3.60
$3	$5.40
$4	$7.20
$5	$8.95
$6	$10.75
$7	$12.60
$8	$14.50
$9	$16.00
$10	$18.00

$15 $26.95

$20 $36.00

Labor Pricing per hour: $60.00

Your crew could then value materials and labor to create an instant invoice so collections can be made at the time of service delivery.

Remember, if you sell what you budgeted for sales, charge for your actual costs and include an appropriate overhead rate and profit *margin*, you must realize the profit you budgeted.

Chapter 10. Establishing an Infrastructure for Business Growth

You've heard it said that the strength of a company lies with its employees. But no employee will ever have your drive and ambition to grow the company. Don't be mad about it. They don't have the stake you have in the success of the business. Just use management tools to motivate, and monitor performance so you can achieve your goals.

Many companies, however, grow without any thought to function or plan. When sales begin to grow, your CPA will emphasize the new tax consequences of the growth without any thought to whether or not the growth can even be sustained. It is incumbent upon the business owner to map out his/her plan to maintain the new growth under a sustainable structure.

What functions will the business perform? Obviously, you will need Sales, Operations, and Administration. Those are the three broad categories you should begin to emphasize in function.

Meeting and securing good people who establish their own value does not constitute building an organization. If you fail to establish your needs, employees will determine their own. If you think I'm wrong, ask any employee if they are doing a good job. They will immediately respond they are. Even the worst employee believes he or she is performing very well, unless, of course, their duties and functions have been defined, and measurements exist to compare their performances to a standard.

Managers, too, need defined parameters to measure performance. Earlier, we indicated one responsibility of managers is to adhere to the budget while accomplishing their tasks. Operations must meet percentage guidelines in managing labor and materials. Administration is responsible for the G&A budget. And sales goals must be met to sustain revenues. Managers must also be able to supervise others to perform duties established for each of them. Each manager must have skills for the jobs to be performed in each segment of the department they run.

In building a new business, sometimes the person we use for a function is simply incapable of being the department manager when things begin to grow. A bookkeeper may not have budgeting and auditing skills available as would a Comptroller who is also a graduate accountant or even a CPA. The bookkeeper may be perfectly suited to operate QuickBooks and to prepare reports and payroll for one or two employees when the business begins. But as payroll clerks, purchasing specialists, accounts payable and receivable clerks, and human resources specialists are added, the manager must be the one emphasizing planning, auditing, and budgeting. A good task performer is not necessarily the best department manager in that instance. The original employee may be suited for multiple tasks, at first, but then more specialized skill is required as hundreds of thousands of dollars of payroll are managed. A mistake at that level could destroy the financial stability of the business.

What should you do? Establish a functional organizational structure which will enable you to grow into a larger organization. As a small business owner, you may have become an entrepreneur after being a good tradesman. You may have been a carpenter who was offered a framing contract by a general contractor who saw your good work ethic. From there, you secured additional jobs until you were in business before you actually decided to be. Your wife helped with bookkeeping and you performed the work. At some point, you must be assured that new jobs will be available when you finish the current job. That means sales. You may have too much work and need help. Sooner or later you will decide to hire a regular crew or even to contract with others to perform bigger jobs. You have become a businessman (maybe without realizing it) and need to establish the structure which will secure the viability of the business for the future.

First we have you! You will either be the President, Managing Partner, or Owner depending upon the entity you choose. Then, we need the three department heads: Administration, Operations, and Sales. At first, you may be all four positions until your revenues grow to a level where additional payroll can be sustained. You may hire the first employees at lower levels on the chart retaining the management level positions for yourself. When sales growth and excess profits become sufficient to add managers, you can either promote and add below the manager, or hire at management level. You decide what position needs to be filled. You decide!

Within each department are positions which need to be defined according to the work they will perform. An example of the various duties is provided to give you some idea of the positions you may need to add as you grow. By properly establishing a **functional** organizational chart, you will not be surprised by growth, and will be able to add essential staff – slotted to assume a specific roll - when you decide it is necessary.

Even service and professional business organizations should do the same thing. An engineer gets a good job with a client and begins his own company. He should map a strategy to grow in order to be able to accept additional work and to sustain the new business.

An example of job duties and a chart follows. It does not have to be elaborate, just available when the work and revenues support the addition of personnel. When you begin to grow, recognize that these positions and duties will have to be accomplished with more skill and efficiency so profits can be maintained in a volatile and competitive environment.

Too often, new owners begin to grow, add staff, and then realize they don't have as much to spend as before. They fail to account for the additional staff in their pricing structure so overhead grows beyond the ability of sales to maintain it. Again, look to percentages for the solution. By maintaining percentages, more funds will be available. If the money you need isn't available even with increased sales, you may have to adjust pricing to provide the funds. Just remember, it's a tight-rope-walk to know when your competitors will follow you or try to "exterminate" you because of your price changes.

Having an infrastructure based upon job function enables you to anticipate needs and to fill them as funds become available.

President

Administration	**Operations**	**Sales/Marketing**

Accounting

   Gen Ledger

   Payables

   Receivables

   Payroll

Taxes

Insurance

Banking

G&A Budget

Petty Cash

Office Supplies

Human Resources

   Hiring/Terminations

   Benefits

   Personnel

Reception

Telephone

Computers

Mail Services

Clerical Duties

Scheduling

Safety

Staffing/Hours

Training

Facilities Maint

Quality Control

Asset Management

COGS Budget

Shipping/Receiving

Revenue Budget

Bids/Quotes

Market Trends

Competition

Customer Service

Prospecting

Marketing

Advertising

Chapter 11. Driving the Business

Armed with the tools you need to properly manage your business, it is now time to drive revenues to achieve growth and to achieve long-term security for your family.

Your CPA is a valuable asset to your professional team, but rarely will discuss with you how to manage your sales budget for growth. He is not an expert in your business and will not understand the finer points of making your business better. That is up to you.

A plumber gets a call from a homeowner with a hot-water heater that has rusted and is leaking water. A crew is dispatched to the site and a new heater has to be installed because the old one has rusted out. A casual review shows that many homes in the neighborhood were built at about the same time and water-heaters may be in the same age and condition.

You contact the neighborhood church and offer them a donation to have their youth group pass out flyers in the neighborhood. For the cost of the flyers and a donation of perhaps $100, you blanket *the neighborhood with flyers describing the water heater problem and a special sale price for replacing them. In your flyer you describe the difference between emergency replacement, with the damage it can cause, versus pre-planed action.*

As a result, you get to change out several more water heaters and residual sales come as others experience the emergency. You have driven sales in a particular neighborhood and even picked up additional work.

Action taken to drive sales is never a mistake. You are in control of your business growth. In every case where work is done, you place a sticker in some pre-planned location (on the water-heater?) so the homeowner can contact you for future work.

If you're in the heating and air-conditioning business, the environment is becoming a major concern. Energy efficiency is being discussed everywhere. And now, thanks to air-tight homes, indoor air pollution is becoming almost a crisis. What a great opportunity exists for the visionary business owner! Adding a segment to your business to install energy management (such as PowerwoRx) products to a home or air-purification into the air ducts can double business revenues. Your existing client base should be contacted to consider these products. In new construction, installation of these devices will add over $1,000 to your sales while enabling the home to be marketed at a much higher selling price.

> *For existing homeowners, new sales of purification systems are revenue producers. An entire industry has been established around air purification and odor/allergy/asthma problems. The new administration has vowed to make energy efficiency and "green" technology a priority. Drive your business to take advantage of the change in public awareness. Mobile home manufacturers should be aware of methods available to eliminate dangerous gasses and odors from construction materials.*

Health-products has grown to become a major industry. Vitamins and food products to enable people to be healthier are available for sale and distribution. Marketing through the internet and express shipping means no boundaries on sales for those who want to expand markets. You would have to be in a cave not to notice the diet food ads on TV. "Losing 40 pounds through eating has never been easier!"

Do you need yellow pages advertising? Yes, you may. But many more will seek you out in the yellow pages "on-line". So you had better be listed there. Macy's closed 11 stores recently. Yet more Americans spend more money every day. Are buying patterns changing? JC Penny thinks so. Their on-line sales have grown exponentially during the last few years.

Traditional home builders have to be cognizant of changes in construction. Following hurricanes Andrew and Katrina, building codes were revamped to require substantial increases in wind tolerance. Steel homes are now available, as are prefabricated cottages and concrete dwellings. Many changes made the cost of building a new home exorbitant. Yet, innovation brings construction back into line and affordable housing can be obtained.

You must have time to plan as a business owner. Your job is to make certain that markets exist for your products and that new markets become available. You must innovate in what you sell, and in how you market your business.

One of the greatest stories of a lack of planning/innovating involves the Swiss manufacturers of watches. Presented with Quartz technology, they dismissed it. The Japanese manufacturers recognized the potential and began making Quartz watches – realizing an amazing market share of watches sold world-wide.

Do not dismiss new technology or innovative techniques of producing your products. If it can be built better, more efficiently, or for less money, it will be done. If your competition can market via the internet, infomercial, or you-tube, it will be done. Change is everywhere and you must be flexible to recognize the value or logic of some of these new methods.

The water heater example from above can be utilized again here. When the plumber received his call, he should already have a place on his form to capture the e-mail addresses of each customer. It's a simple thing to ask for an e-mail address when asking for the name and address of the customer. Later, after the crisis is solved, an e-mail thank you can be sent to the homeowner. You can even ask them to participate in a small survey to help you improve. Ask them how they found your company during the crisis. Have they been asked about your work by other neighbors? How did you rate the performance of the work crew? Were they clean and efficient? Were they polite?

Later still, a marketing e-mail can be sent inviting the homeowner to purchase additional services. The plumber may partner with a manufacturer to provide instant hot water as an economical method of providing heated water for the home. It could pay for itself through energy savings and may even be eligible for tax credits. You may partner with the gas company to provide an additional gas hookup outdoors for outdoor grilling or seafood boils.

There are many ways to harness your existing customer base. But to perform work and not plan to market to the same customers in the future is a giant, GIANT mistake. If every sale had to come from a new customer, we would be out of business after a time. Repeat business enables us to grow from one level to the next.

Driving your business means having the ability and foresight to anticipate methods of securing new business when circumstances present themselves. You have the same tools available that everyone else has. Be creative and innovative. But most importantly, do something; and, when you do, give it a chance to work. Don't abandon the action if you don't see immediate results.

Chapter 12. Achieving a CEO Mindset

Can your business run when you aren't there? It can if you have a CEO mindset. Many business owners feel they have to manage every aspect of their employee's time. They have to know everything that's going on at every minute. This attitude stifles business innovation and limits activities and expression among employees.

The successful CEO employs good employees and allows them to perform to the best of their creative ability. Sometimes they even make mistakes. Often they don't do things the way you would have, and occasionally they do it better.

I once knew the owner of a large CPA firm. He was very successful as the owner and manager of the firm even though he wasn't a CPA himself. He employed the best CPAs he could find and they performed dutifully for the clients of the firm. He didn't know the tax law as they knew it. And he wasn't able to perform certain types of audits, personally. But his CPAs could do anything the client needed. His special benefit to the firm was that he could market the services and continue finding clients to provide billable time for those who worked for him. He was also able to manage the G&A budget and the bottom line.

There are two specific management tools needed to be a successful CEO.

- **Reporting systems** to enable the information you need to be presented to you. It can be verbal or written, but you need to know what your people are doing through accurate and complete reporting.

- **Delegation** is an essential tool of every successful CEO. Once you know what must be done, you must give the responsibility of that task to a person qualified to perform it. He/she must do it and report on its accomplishment. You must *stay out of the way* unless asked a question on method or budget.

If you acquire these two basic skills, you may be able to find time for planning and training those subordinates to perform the next job. A carpenter who continues to swing the hammer will not have time to market; review reports; plan and schedule workers; find the best price on materials; budget and seek variances in the budget; and employ new workers. Yet that same carpenter will allow his crew to be short-handed since he scheduled himself as one of the crew members and is now distracted by his other duties.

I once consulted with a company that had two distinct business operations. The manufacturing division prepared materials for construction in homes and commercial offices. The other was a construction entity which installed the materials. The owner personally managed the construction entity while his younger brother managed the manufacturing entity.

The manufacturing entity was in turmoil due to changes in daily scheduling. The older brother, the owner, would use the manufacturing facility to draw extra employees as needed for the construction business. This left the younger brother with a constant problem of trying to perform his manufacturing duties without some of his scheduled employees. That was tough to cope with yet, it wasn't the only problem. The older brother also re-scheduled some of the jobs which made the younger brother insignificant to his own employees. It undermined his influence and killed his effectiveness.

To solve the problem, I had to stop the owner from interfering in the manufacturing process. He had to get a daily report, work out changes with the younger brother, and leave him alone to handle the manufacturing duties. Any employee who bypassed the younger brother for guidance had to be re-routed to the younger brother. This helped re-establish a chain of command and afforded the younger brother a chance to meet schedules and to manage his employees. He was actually quite competent and was able to demonstrate that to his older brother who became comfortable with the delegation and reporting process. Each company began to grow.

As stated elsewhere, we are able to communicate today as never before. With cell phones and satellite phones we can speak in real time from anywhere in the world. We have internet and e-mail which enables written reports to be delivered in real time. There is no reason for a business owner to be without reports. To manage a company requires only that

- reporting be timely, accurate, and consistent.
- That supervisors and managers have some basic skill and desire to manage for profit.

- That each person be assigned specific responsibilities. And, that
- owners let them perform without interference.

Performed under these guidelines, a business owner will have the time and opportunity to implement new ideas and innovations. He will be able to accurately shift his company to seize opportunities for growth and security in any economy.

Section Three: Secret to Success

In the book "God is My CEO" Larry Julian writes that a man's life work can be divided in half. The first half is concerned with becoming **_successful._** The second is consumed with becoming **_significant_**.

Those I've met who recognize that God is the source of success attain significance earlier than those who do not. It is uncommon to hear of ethics and morals in business unless one is bashing a company that has neither. On the news, we are told of evil corporations and CEO's who pay or receive too much compensation for being successful. We hear of evil bankers who oppress the borrowers of home mortgages. Are they immoral? Are they unethical?

I've just explained how to protect your profits. Are following these principles immoral or unethical? My faith and reading tell me emphatically that they are not.

Morals and ethics in business begin with telling the truth. Being truthful with employees, customers, and investors is paramount to long-term success. Disclosure of vital information is not only smart, it is lawful and moral.

Protecting Profits in Any Economy

Business owners must always remember that treating others with respect and caring is not only good Christian values, it is good business sense. Earlier I spoke of the differences between bonuses and incentives. When an employee has an opportunity to earn an incentive, he responds with added effort and respect for the owner. Bonuses afford him the opportunity for neither respect nor achievement. A good principle, therefore, is to enable the employee to earn an incentive and to help grow a moral environment in the workplace built upon mutual respect.

Customers should be treated with empathy and respect. Put yourself into a customer's shoes and view your offering from his perspective. If you were that customer, would you buy the product or service? Would the value be there for what is being offered? Does your product or service solve a problem or provide a new convenience? Is there a reason for him/her to purchase the item?

In selling a product or service, I never worry that the price is too high. God has never said what too much profit may be. Some can make 800% profit and retain a market. Others can sell an item with a 4% mark-up and fight for every sale. From a customer's viewpoint, the profit margin is unimportant. The product must have value for the customer.

When I had my grocery store, my partner was constantly pointing out the customer attitude toward neighborhood vendors. The same person who would pay $2.50 for a hot dog at a sporting event fussed at paying 69 cents for one at our store. It wasn't the hot dog quality, it was the idea of venue. But it wasn't immoral to charge $2.50 at the sporting event, either.

Recently, the media began making a big "to do" out of the billions of profit dollars being made by oil companies. The reply from several companies was that the billions only amounted to 8% profit, and that the amount was large because the total volume was large. Now, with falling prices, no one seems concerned that 8% is reasonable since their own purchase is more affordable. If oil companies would have lowered prices to make product more affordable, they would have done so at the expense of their stockholders, employees and customers. Lower profits would not have offered long-term stability. It would have jeopardized the availability of a basic commodity we all seem to desperately need. In all of the chastisement, the government tax rate wasn't discussed. That rate exceeds 40% in almost every state. There was no outcry demanding government take less – only the evil oil companies who provide the commodity.

Business owners should never allow any outsider to choose a moral code for them. If we allowed People for the Ethical Treatment of Animals (PETA) to choose the moral code for our lifestyles, none of us would drink milk, or eat cheese, or meat. Yet, God said, *"Every moving thing that liveth shall be meat for you; even as the green herb have I given you all things."* (Gen 9:3) There are numerous "moralists" who know nothing about morals or ethics. It is because their moral code does not come from God.

Timeless, moral standards can be found in the Bible. They were provided to us by a benevolent God who wants us to follow His principles for a happy, healthy life on earth. Sure he wants us to choose His Son as Savior so we can be with Him in eternity. And, eternal life is ours simply by believing. But applying the principles of the Bible is available to those who don't believe, as well. Why would you apply them? Because they work!

One great example of a Biblical Principle that works, is the example of giving. The Bible cautions not to rob God of His tithe (10%). (Micah 3:10-12). Profits are the results of a lot of hard work, planning, and execution on the part of many well-trained and experienced employees.

> *But there are many circumstances which are way beyond the control of any of us. There is health, economic, credit, governmental, environmental and other concerns which you certainly cannot predict. A business rocking along in New Orleans during 2005 could not have predicted the fallout from Hurricane Katrina. And, I'm not saying that if you fail to give you will get a hurricane. But I sold my home and moved to another state in July of 2005. One month later, the neighborhood from which I moved was devastated by Katrina. No business was conducted for quite some time. No telephone service existed for weeks. I was protected during a time of crisis for many. I give thanks to God for that protection.*

In describing charity, Matthew writes as a quote from Christ, "...*Inasmuch as you have done it unto the least of these my brethren, you have done it unto me.* " (Mat 25:40) According to this statement, it would seem to indicate that tithing to a church or synagogue is not required to comply with Micah 3: 10-12. Businesses are confronted by solicitors from every direction. E-mail, direct mail, walk-ins, etc are constantly seeking a donation or ad in some flyer or magazine. And, if you give to one, you are then bombarded with additional mailings seeking more from them and other organizations. They have become so well organized and devoted to getting whatever change is in your pocket, that nationally, a "do not call list" was initiated and laws passed to keep them from soliciting you by telephone.

But you should give back. That's the principle being offered and one you should immediately consider. Read the biographies of Colgate, or Hershey. Each of these individuals ended up tithing as much as 90% of his income. They each attributed their willingness to give back a tithe as the reason for their good fortunes.

Give your time and a percentage of your profits to those who are truly in need and you will receive a personal and financial reward for your effort. That is guaranteed by Micah 3:10-12 (Old Testament) and again in Matthew 25:40 (New Testament). You will gain financially and in personal significance. Recognizing that every success is not attributable to your own wisdom but that some is based upon the will of God, will instill a sense of humility to your good fortune to temper your own pride. You will gain success and significance, the two qualities everyone seeks in business.

In conclusion, be moral and ethical in your dealing with employees, customers and investors. Learn to apply the principles contained in this book to sustain and to protect profits. And, when profits appear, recognize that some factors outside of your own capabilities were also significant in helping them to occur. Give a tithe from your profits to those in need – religious, civic, and/or individual.

Protecting Profits in Any Economy

Made in the USA
Charleston, SC
20 June 2011